Hi Neighbor
Archie Lieberman

I am thankful for my neighbors and my family—my wife, Esther and Mama Rose, L.B.K., Eric, Mary Kay, Taylor, Seth, Bob, Julie, Noah, Kurt, Bernard, Buzzie, Paul and June; and Jim Diehl, Dave Reis. Their inspiration and support is a part of this work and it is to them that this book is dedicated.

And I wish to acknowledge the photographic print work of Jack Leblebjian and Sahag Gamilian; Lena Tabori for her talents and for her constant friendship and faith in the project; John Hart who edited this work with his very special integrity, sensitivity and truthfulness; and Jenny Barry, the designer, who found so many wonderful ways to orchestrate the work. The excitement together in the crucible of production left me with great respect for them, for their work, and, indeed, for them as neighbors.

First published in the USA in 1993 by Collins Publishers San Francisco
Copyright © 1993 Archie Lieberman
Design: Jennifer Barry
Editor: John Hart
Production Managers: Jonathan Mills and Lynne Noone
Design and Production Assistants: Cecile Chronister and Kristen Wurz
Library of Congress Cataloging-in-Publication Data:
Lieberman, Archie.
p. cm.
Includes index.
ISBN 0-00-255209-4
1. Scales Mound (Ill.)--Pictorial works. 2. Scales Mound (Ill.)--Social life and customs.
I. Title.
F549.S43L54 1993
977.3'343--dc20 CIP 93-3554
All rights reserved, including the right of reproduction in whole
or in part or in any form.
Printed in Italy by Arnaldo Mondadori LTD. 10 9 8 7 6 5 4 3 2 1

Photo Captions
Cover: Bill Hammer, Jr.
Page 1: Dick Morhardt and his gas station.
Pages 2-3: Schapville neighbors in front of Anton Schap's
blacksmith shop, July 4, 1974.
Pages 6-7: Dusty road.

NEIGHBORS

A Forty-Year Portrait of an American Farm Community

By Archie Lieberman

Collins Publishers San Francisco

A Division of HarperCollins*Publishers*

PROLOGUE: THE LAND AND ITS PAST

There is serenity now in a place I know like no other. It is around Scales Mound in the deeply etched panorama of Jo Daviess County, in the northwest corner of Illinois, where the land is crayon green in the spring and fleece white in the winter and stays that way until the thaw. Its hills and valleys are sectioned past a thousand horizons with woods and contoured farm fields. There is fish and game. The air smells good. No jet planes scream in the sky, the major highways are two-lane blacktops uncluttered by billboards, and small rivers run under the planks of backroad bridges. The people are kind, go to church, pursue virtue, work hard with the land, and cling to their families. From all these things they harvest contentment.

In the creation, in what was destined to become this place, shallow seas were formed. In cycles of millions of years of submergence and retreat, strata of sediment were deposited. In one period, lead bearing dolomite was laid down. Then dry land appeared and it was carved into valleys and ridges. Then great ice drifts came and scraped away nine-tenths of the ruggedness from the Illinois landscape. But these glaciers slipped past Jo Daviess County, leaving it as it was formed in the beginning.

Now the stage was set for mankind. Asians first, fifty thousand years before the empires of Europe established fringes of culture on the new world's shores. For the French, the first Europeans to come around here, exploration gained them Indian friendships and vast lands which they dotted with pleasant settlements and beautiful-sounding names. In 1721 they searched for silver, but found only lead and, disappointed, most of them left. One hundred years later, lead diggings would make this the scene of the country's first big mining rush and Galena, the center of it all, would be turned overnight into a city of thirty thousand canvas and bark tents. "There is no civil law here," complained one Massachusetts man. By 1832 a semblance of order came, marred only briefly by Black Hawk, the war chief of the Sauk and Fox Indians. A volunteer army, which included Abraham Lincoln, was mustered. The wars ended when the army massacred Black Hawk's people. The next year the tribes ceded all their land to the state of Illinois and moved west. The Indian was gone from Illinois.

Out of chaos, struggle, the colonial revolution, and the push westward, the American character was shaped and it now shaped the land. In 1818 Illinois became a state that included the hills of Galena and Jo Daviess County, named for a Kentuckian who died a hero fighting in the 1811 Battle of Tippecanoe.

In 1673, near here, above the point where Illinois now meets with Wisconsin and Iowa, its carved bluffs piercing the Mississippi River, Jacques Marquette, an exploring French priest, made the first wonderstruck reports on the vistas which lay before his astonished eyes. He noted the existence of lead, the fertility of the land, and the variety of game. It was an open invitation to adventurers: the French *coureurs de bois*, trappers, frontiersmen, lead miners, speculators, soldiers, and fortune hunters. Finally, farmers came to this wilderness. To them, to be good was to be independent, rugged, hardworking, and never betraying. These were an uncommon people of dreams, who, though they loved the virgin lands, could blink their eyes and see tilled fields, nice houses, stock grazing, and a good water supply.

The Latin word for lead gave Galena, the county seat, its name, and lead made it into a river boomtown. Samuel Scales built a post house alongside a mound by a stagecoach trail. The town of Scales Mound, only ten miles away from Galena on the stagecoach line, was on the edge of the frontier, but Galena itself was the rich metropolis of the Northwest. The prosperous days of Galena ended suddenly. The surface veins of lead ran out, the gold rush of '49 lured people away, and the Galena River began to silt in, making the channel to the Mississippi unnavigable for cargo boats. Jo Daviess County settled into farming.

With Europe still shaken by the Napoleonic wars, migration continued. Guidebooks told the immigrant of Illinois rivers, of land where corn had grown on inexhaustible soil for one hundred years, of game and abundant wild fruit of all kinds, of farmers with several hundred hogs, two hundred cattle, twenty horses, a thousand sheep. English, Irish, and German families, wanting to be free of their remaining feudal obligations, migrated to the county and settlements became villages and towns. In America they could find freedom and unlimited land and could prosper by working hard. In 1852 in Jo Daviess County, only a little of the edge of the wilderness had been dulled. The source of the Mississippi had not yet been discovered. The railroad owned two million acres and was selling it at five to twenty dollars an acre.

Like the heads of the families Hoppe, Schap, Grube, Boettner, and Eversoll of that time, John Rudolph Hammer, a farmer from Saxony, Germany, took his family from the German countryside and migrated to America. They went west over historic trails, the past entering into them as they entered into Illinois country. When they reached Scales Mound in 1852 they bought railroad land. In one year Scales Mound would be a town, in three the railroad would arrive, and in eight the Civil War would begin. Theo Hoppe and Anton Schap, barely able to speak English, volunteered and spent four years in a blue uniform. Both were from the area that became Schapville.

John Rudolph Hammer brought his family to a place that rolled into the bottom land of a creek in a hidden valley fifteen miles from Galena and three from Scales Mound. He came to farm. Like the others, Hammer subdued the land with ax and plow. He built a house and, with three other men, founded a church. Five generations, echoes of his spirit, came after him. His son, Bernhardt, fathered nine children. Of Bernhardt's children, George Hammer became the father of Willis Hammer. Willis Hammer became the father of Willis Hammer, Jr. Willis Hammer, Jr., became the father of James Alan Hammer, born 110 years after John Rudolph Hammer reached Illinois country. Of the six generations, none rooted far from the old homestead.

It is with the Willis Hammer family and their neighbors that this book is concerned. For forty years I have witnessed, in friendship and with a camera, the births and agings of three generations. When I asked, a neighbor told me that I was allowed to make pictures because "it was your work and we did not want to deprive you of earning your living."

A little beyond John Rudolph Hammer's homestead, the Willis Hammer homeplace lies in the seclusion of a hollow. On land laced by roller-coaster gravel roads, you go up ridges, down into valleys, and along river bottoms. Cattle and horses graze, hawks circle, jackrabbits dart into the road. In the woods, although you cannot see them, are deer. The winters are hard, long, and cold. The growing season is less than five months. When it is winter and the air is frigid, at a distance red barns are like linoleum patches on a background of brilliant snow, and you can see puffs of breath coming from a farmer doing his chores. All is crisp and pure.

On such a winter day in 1954, over a hundred years after John Rudolph Hammer homesteaded, his great-great-grandson, Billy Hammer, aged thirteen, waited to meet me on his back road, which butted into the blacktop that covered the old stage line. He smiled an easy greeting. His sister, Janet, had won a national sewing contest and I

had come to photograph her for a magazine. Billy led me into the generations of his family's storybook landscape. Mildred, Bill, Sr., Janet, and Billy made me feel comfortable immediately. I did my work, ate delicious food, and thought about coming back to recapture the wonderful feelings I got from them.

When summer came I revisited the Hammers. To my surprise, Billy had grown almost a whole head taller. His joy in life had increased proportionately. I made a picture of him walking alongside his father, who was driving the tractor. That struck off an idea: One day I would make a picture of Billy and his son in the same way.

In the years that followed, as Billy grew, I was also covering depressing stories, but when I came out to the Hammers joy returned. After one of my closest friends was killed photographing a war I went out to the farm to reassure myself that the world, somewhere, still made sense.

In the morning the sun rises over the ridge and you truly know the day has begun. Roosters really crow, cows moo, pigs oink, church bells toll, and streams swish and gurgle. People work, pray, and play. They crochet doilies, quilt, can food, bake wonderful cakes, and eat well. The ground smells the way ground should, the tractor groans power, the manure spreader enriches the earth, the bees fly to clover, a neighbor on a dusty road waves as he passes in a pickup, the hay is sweet, the scent of silage is slightly intoxicating, the farm dog runs barking alongside the sheep or cattle he herds, the crickets sing, the birds go about their business. Everything goes about its business in a natural way. In the evening the sun goes down over another ridge, and you know you have lived a sensible day.

That is why I welcomed the call I got from Millie Hammer: "I just heard in church tonight that the old Hoppe farm is for sale. You better come out. It's just the right place for you!"

We bought the Hoppe farm in 1973. In 1983 we moved to the farm full-time so I could be more close, more involved, more of a neighbor, more of the time. And continue my work here.

Our place is about fifteen miles from Galena, seven miles from Scales Mound, and a mile away from Schapville, a village of twenty-four houses, fifty people, two churches, and two cemeteries, Presbyterian and Lutheran.

Perhaps it is an imperfect theory, but I have always thought that the land forms the character and look of a people. I believe that my neighbors take on the strong, reliable, and kind characteristics of their landscape.

What follows is a selection of words from four decades of conversation and photographs from 58,584 exposures on 35 millimeter film. This may not be exactly how things were. This is how things seemed to me, a reflection of my profound feelings in those 58,584 moments which, without compromise, usurped my attention: something in the land and the crops, the neighbors, the seasons, the troubles, the births and the deaths, time—which passed too quickly—and the land which has no sharp edges, where everything has rounded corners and where everything, even in the worst of situations, seems forgiving. Just like my neighbors.

—Archie Lieberman, Schapville, Illinois. April 3, 1993.

Left: Willis Hammer, Sr. and Bill Hammer, Jr. They are known as Old Bill and Young Bill.

Above: Janet Hammer modeling the dress which won her a sewing contest. And which brought me to meet the Hammers in 1954. In the background on the homeplace porch is her father, Willis Hammer, Sr.

Cletus Hammer

Carol and Clint Youle moving an old farm house to its new location.

Tommy Wasmund and Tammy Stadel riding the school bus from Schapville to Scales Mound.

Stanley "Jackie" Duerr

Carmen Panico

Russell Maughan, Elizabeth banker.

Curly and Marie Eversoll, Henry Hoppe, and Ernie Boettner. New Year's Eve.

Irwin Bishop of Bishop's Busy Big Store.

Cousins Oliver and Lou Koester

Skip Schwerdtfeger

Cal Menzemer and granddaughter.

Mrs. Wenzel in her Scales Mound greenhouse.

Orrin Simmons

Sarge Stegall (Ricky's father)

Archie celebrates his birthday with neighbors.

Henry Johnson, horse breeder and trainer.

Ernie Boettner

Aerial view of Schapville.

John Eversoll (Curly Eversoll's nephew) kissing Mildred "Ma" Stadel.

John Eversoll, grandson of old Jack Eversoll.

Dorothy Hammer at her baby shower.

Ernie Boettner with David and Peggy Grube.

Evelyn and Meldon Grube with family and friends at the annual Grube family picnic.

Bill Brickner with daughters Bonnye and Brenda.

Paul and Helen Kindig

After the Civil War, Theo Hoppe settled about two miles south of where Anton Schap set up his blacksmith shop. The sons followed in the fathers' work, Henry Hoppe as farmer and Tony Schap, Jr. as blacksmith, and continued to live and work together as neighbors. The hilly road the Hoppes took into the new settlement is now Hoppe Road and it intersects with Schapville Road in what is now Schapville.

After he retired from farming, Henry Hoppe moved into the village next door to Curly and Marie Eversoll and across the road from the Presbyterian church where he mows the grass these days around the church and in the cemetery.

Marie Eversoll always refers to him as Mr. Hoppe. A lot of his neighbors, with respect and affection, call him Hank.

Henry Hoppe

Henry Hoppe, 84, is talking about how his father Theo Hoppe came to Scales Mound and the Schapville area where the Hoppes grew hay, corn, and oats for the dairy herd they kept on 340 acres of the homeplace Theo settled before the Civil War. Henry Hoppe was born there and so were all eight of his children. He has twenty-three grandchildren and thirteen great-grandchildren. He started plowing with horses when he was nine years old.

HENRY HOPPE: He come from Germany. I ain't quite sure what the name of it was. He told me different times, but I don't know. It's Hiddleburg something. I don't remember. Except that it was a little country, little villages, you know, they all lived there to-

gether. They farmed. They was living in, well, they said they lived in town and then they had to go out on the farm to work. They come here about 1850—it must have been—because that was be-fore the Civil War. If this was the first place he come to, I don't know.

This was all railroad land. So he probably bought it then because it was far from the railroad and didn't cost too much. This was all wild country when they come here.

He was a man something like me. He don't talk too much. Like I say I ain't much of a talker myself. He was always a quiet man who took everything in. In the Civil War time he was in the army for four years.

I had two brothers and five sisters. Oh, there was Charlie, John, and myself. Then there was Elizabeth, then Minnie, Mary, Josephine, and Esther. I'm the only one left. And the Civil War was in '64, wasn't it somewhere around like that? Now I don't know much of what happened; they never spoke, always that they lived here. They grew up and the trees grew up.

He was a hard worker like the rest of them. He didn't get to be a rich man. He built up all these buildings. He had a little left. My father had a gold piece he saved, that $5.00 piece. He had that when he died. I'd say he had about $4,000 when he died. He was a rich man then.

(The homestead is on a hill just above the creek. The homeplace is partially log, and there is a barn and a corn crib.)

That's where I was born. I lived there. I was born and raised there. I still lived there when I took the farm over. And then a few years afterwards, I moved over to where you live now. You see my boys was big enough then. They tried their hand at it and never was satisfied and moved away for better money. So. *(No one lived at the home-place after that.)*

(I asked if he saw the truth of the Bible.)

Well, yeah. Oh yes. You seem to think more and live it more. You know, when you're young, you don't pay so much attention to it. I'll admit that I didn't either. But now you've got more time to think and realize what's ahead of you. And what's in back of you, and what you did and what you didn't do. And what you should've done.

I was the one that really started the English language down here at the Lutheran church. They brought it up. There were so many younger ones coming up, you know, they had one English service a month. And when it was brought up I made a motion to adopt it and they was pretty mad at me.

Page 14: The Hoppe homestead homeplace. Recently sold, the homeplace was burned down by the Elizabeth Fire Department in a training exercise.

Left: Henry Hoppe in his Schapville house.

Above: Henry Hoppe with some of his family.

In one way or another a lot of the neighbors around here—Curly and Marie Eversoll through the Winters family, Meldon Grube and Ernie Boettner through the Arnolds—are related to Anton Schap, the founder of Schapville.

Haldor Schap is Anton's grandson. Haldor is a jack-of-all-trades. He worked as a cook and waiter in an Elizabeth restaurant in the 1930s, worked on the railroad in the 1940s, sold Chevrolets in the 1950s, and later was John Balbach's auction clerk. Now he works in real estate at Carol and Skip Schwerdtfeger's firm.

"In Jo Daviess County everybody knows Hal, there is only one Hal," says his son Gary, an Illinois state trooper.

HALDOR SCHAP

"Corporal Anton Schap, after whom Schapville was named," a history book says, "has done more for this town than any other man. He is a large-hearted, whole-souled gentleman, very liberal and public spirited, obliging and courteous, a man of more than ordinary abilities, with a sensitive nature and cultivated tastes."

John Anton Christian Schap was born September 12, 1812, in Hieldburghausen, Saxony. By the time he was seventeen he was already a painter, a sculptor, and a blacksmith, and had migrated to the United States.

In the city of Baltimore he lost the little money he had by being overcharged on his ticket to Chicago; his final destination was Galena, at the time a more important city. After missing trains, suffering hunger, and wandering about Galena, he finally found his sister, Mrs. Arnold, in Guilford Township and went to work as a blacksmith with Henry Winter. When the Civil War broke out he was one of the first to enlist at Galena and saw action at Chickamauga, Lookout Mountain, Chattanooga, and Atlanta. In one skirmish he was slightly wounded. After the war he married Maria Winter. They lived in Galena for a year, and in 1867 they moved near Mill Creek in Thompson Township. He started a blacksmith shop on his farm, and the village of Schapville grew up around it. He and Maria had ten children. One of these children was Anton, Jr., who was also an artist and a blacksmith and was the father of Haldor.

HALDOR SCHAP: I have always admired the picture of the village blacksmith where he's got the horse out at the head of building.

In the old blacksmith shop we had three stoves, in order to keep that big old shop warm; in the house we had the cookstove in the kitchen and we had stoves in the two other front rooms. Dad used to go out and contract a two-acre piece of ground. We would cut off the wood and cut it into pole length and stack it. And then when we got this all stacked we took out all the stumps and we used the ground for two years for potatoes. At the end of two years you had the roots pretty well worked out and then it would go back into agriculture ground. And then we'd take another two-acre tract. But we cut the wood one year into pole length. The next year it was sawed into firewood size, and the third year we'd haul it home and he'd pick out the nice chunks that we split for the cookstove and the chunks with the knots in, the big ones, went into the blacksmith shop as firewood and the smaller ones that weren't quite so big went into the house.

I worked in the blacksmith shop and I learned how to do everything except to the point where Dad would say, "Watch that horse walk in the door."

And when he got inside Dad would say, "How did he walk in?"

I said, "On four feet."

My dad was German and he would say, "You dummer hazel (dumb jackass)."

Because he wanted me to see how that horse was stepping and that is the big secret of blacksmithing—to watch a horse walk in the door and know what you are going to do with his feet. Soon as we would get them in, I would pull his shoes off and then Dad would trim the foot properly, so you'd get a step properly.

At one time they got fifty cents for a reset and a dollar for new shoes, then it went up to seventy-five cents for a reset and, I think, a dollar and a quarter for new shoes. And that's about the highest he ever got. Now they get about sixteen. Four dollars a foot.

My dad was an artist. And then he also got into veterinarian work. A guy'd come in and say, "My horse has got a sore mouth." Well they had what they call lambers. It was kind of a rib plate. And we had irons and we'd put it in their mouth and then we'd sear them with hot irons. Sometime you'd get a horse in and you'd file his teeth down.

When we used to get shoes we had to turn the heels on them, and then wintertime, when I first started at the shop, I stood on a chair. Our shoes came blank as far as concerned the holes for 'never slip corks,' and I stood on a stool and I had to crank that bit where we tapped the threads in the shoes. Then I would take them over to the vise where we had a special holder for the shoe where I would screw the corks in. That's where I first started out. I was too small—I had to stand on a chair in order to get up high enough so I could work them. That's where I started. From there I just kept on going.

Page 18: Gary Schap, an Illinois state trooper, poses with a picture of his great-grandfather, Anton Schap, founder of Schapville.

Left: Haldor Schap, grandson of Anton Schap, and father of Gary.

Following pages: Aerial landscape of Schapville, facing east. The road at the bottom leads to Ernie Boettner's farm. At the corner on the right side of the Presbyterian Church is the Eversoll house. To the left of the church is Young Bill Hammer's land.

The Hammer family has lived here since the 1850s. The Hammers never spend much time in town except to go to church, the bank, and the store, but their presence is very much felt. When Willis "Bill" Hammer renders an opinion, it is acted on, as when he mentioned at a township meeting that because more people were traveling on Hoppe Road it was hard to get over the 'Coon Creek overpass. The road was widened there, so two cars could cross at the same time.

Mildred's cheerful ways with her neighbors make her a favorite among them and when she says something it can be taken as gospel. She has a way with words and phrases that clears the air.

WHAT IT MEANS TO LOVE THE LAND

For most of his life, Willis Hammer, Sr. has been working hard on the land, milking cows twice a day and fighting the extremes of nature and market prices in the valley in which he was born and which he has never left. Three generations of Hammer men before him knew this land and maybe his children and grandchildren will, too. He is sparing with words.

BILL, SR.: We used to milk twenty, twenty-five cows in the early days. Now we're milking seventy to eighty. I still enjoy it all. I'd sooner milk than anything. Why?

Mildred Evans Hammer grew up on a farm near Shullsburg, Wisconsin and has been Bill's wife since he brought her to the valley. She has worked hard alongside him in the yard, house, and field, and in raising their two children.

MILDRED: Why? Because you love farming, because you love someone. Before we got machines, I helped him milk by hand out there in the yard. I'd shove one cow out of the way and sit down to another one. In summertime, we wouldn't even put them in the barn, we'd put them in the yard. It would be, "Bill, did you milk this one?" "Yep," and I'd shove her out of the way. "Did you milk that one?" When we were first married, we were eight years over to the Hesselbachers' working there. We've been only here and over the field to there and back. Sure, there's been lots of hard work. You either love farming or get out of it.

BILL, SR.: I heard someone once say that Americans love the land like they love their own skin, and they love work in the same way. I think that's one of the things of being a farmer. You love the land, to plant things and see them grow, and you enjoy the hard work that goes with it. That's farming. I think any farmer loves the land. I don't think you'd ever make a good farmer unless you really enjoyed doing it or working with it.

MILDRED: The land is like a child. It's like a revolving thing. As a child, you grow up with the land and it takes care of you, and then one day you plant and it grows as a child does and you take care of it.

Like his mother and father, Bill, Jr. has worked hard with the land in the same place all his life. While most young people in rural areas must go elsewhere to find their opportunities, Bill, Jr. can farm.

BILL, JR.: Out here it's always changing; it's always different or doing something different. No day is exactly the same. It's a challenge and it's a recycling. Each spring you start plowing, planting, then it grows, you harvest; it's just a constant recycle. The land for me is a way of living, of being free and independent. You're not just working for a paycheck.

What I really like about it is when you're alone, like when you spray corn. You're by yourself and you're just constantly looking at a beautiful picture. It isn't the same every day. The trees are blowing different, there's fresh

Page 24: The Hammer homeplace.

Left: *(from left to right)* The senior Hammers, Willis and Mildred; The junior Hammers, Bill and Dorothy, with Judy and Jim.

Above: Jim Hammer, age 10, running alongside the tractor and kicker baler holding the first cut hay.

air and the different seasons. I can spend sixteen hours by myself and not talk to anybody. I mean, I like being alone. I wouldn't like being completely alone. I like my family around. That's enough.

A farmer is someone who likes to work and enjoys seeing stuff grow. That keeps him on the land. And the time goes fast; sometimes you don't even know what day of the week it is, and you're always surprised that one season is over and another is here.

Farmers do a lot of grumbling. But you have to work the land because it's what you got. You can't really get mad at it and expect something from it. The land only does what you do to it. If you don't take care of it, it won't take care of you. You got to like it. Just like the animals. You got to like them and pamper them. The same way as the land. You got to love it all. Like a day that we might like for ourselves isn't the proper day for growing corn. A good miserable humidity day, hot, where you can hardly stand it, is a perfect day for growing corn. That's nature, and it's sort of a partner in all you do. Everything will turn out all right anyhow. If the Lord wants it that way, I guess that's the way it's going to have to be.

Dorothy, Bill, Jr.'s wife, also grew up on a farm near Scales Mound.

DOROTHY: To me the farm is the land. I love the farm because it's someplace that's just ours. It's what we make our living off. Bill likes to climb up a hill in the summer and sometimes I go with him. You look down and see those fields you've planted and worried over, and they're growing good. You feel good. It's beautiful, the gold of the oats and the green of the corn.

BILL, SR.: When you see things growing, growing up out of seeds, you know all you could do was plant them and take care of them. It's impossible for a human to make seeds without the help of Him. You make a tractor out of a lot of artificial stuff, but you can't make all the different kinds of plant seeds.

MILDRED: One of the best explanations I ever heard was at Sunday school. Once, when a child said he didn't know if there was a God or not, the teacher got kind of provoked and she said, "You mean to tell me that you can put a little black seed in the ground and you'll get a red plant with a white center and a green top, which is a radish, and you don't believe in God? Nothing else could do it!" There's a lot of them that don't go to church and they might say they don't believe in God. What is it they don't believe in then?

Cletus Hammer, a cousin, sat on his porch railing on a summer evening just before evening milking. From his hillside house, where his grandfather, Bernhardt Hammer, had laid fieldstone to make an embankment, he could see far into the valleys and hills of the county. Below him was Mill Creek. Cletus' wife, Wilma, had just brought the cows to the barn.

CLETUS: Right down over there, along the creek, my great-grandfather Rudolph went and settled. He was the first owner of the land to do anything with it after the railroad let loose of the land. My dad never traveled far and I don't have to. We have so many kinds of recreation right on our own farm.

WILMA: Cletus has never been anyplace else. This is where he has always been. His roots are really planted here.

CLETUS: That's true. But I think I love this land, all right. To me the land is my being. It's all I've got. It's my existence. I feel like I'm just a part of it. When you read in the Bible where it says God gave you this land to till it, to take care of it, to prosper, that's what it means to me. It's my duty to do this. I don't consider it a job exactly. It's a duty. A responsibility. That gives me my happiness and satisfaction and a reason for being here.

Right: Old Bill Hammer feeding cattle in the snow. The homeplace is in the background.

Following pages: Bill Hammer, Jr. alongside a tractor driven by his father. This was the moment I asked myself, "What if I continued to photograph the Hammers until Bill, Jr. has a son, then at the appropriate time, photograph all three in the same way?" It was the beginning of this book.

29

By the time Willis Hammer, Jr. was fourteen, he was known as Junior, Butch, Billy, and Bill. Work has always been a joy to him because he was outside and with his father. Unhappiness is not natural to him. He has always had chores. At three he fed the dog and followed his father around; at six he got the cows out of the pasture; at nine he milked, even though he was still

not strong enough to lift the fifty-pound milk bucket; at ten, though his mother worried about the hills, he was driving the tractor; by the time he was twelve, he could do a man's work; and at thirteen he made a motorscooter, using wheelbarrow wheels and a chain-saw engine, and rode it to chase cattle when he wasn't rounding them up on a horse.

Until the seventh grade, he walked a mile to a one-room country schoolhouse, where Ruth Boettner taught the eight students. That was abandoned the next year for a consolidated school in Scales Mound. Billy didn't like school. It took him away from the real world on the farm. He joined the Boy Scouts but attended only three meetings. "That was for kids who don't have anything to do."

A neighbor recalled: "When Butch was little, about three he started, he was allowed to take a horse and follow his dad all the time. Always with his dad on an old horse. He just followed his dad, just to be with him. He learned a lot. No matter what Old Bill would be doing, Butch'd know what was going on."

BILL, JR.: I liked being around him. It was fun learning to do things I saw him do, to respect him and what he was doing, and I'd want to learn the job, too. Then the day came when he'd let me do something. Then in a year I'd be a little older and he'd start me in on something new. It was a joy learning and thinking that you're a man before you really are. If I was figuring that I was throwing bales on like a man, I'd throw twice as hard. There are things about farm life that might seem like work, but they're fun. We used to burn wood, so I had to put wood in the wood box and if I wasn't busy with chores, I could find other things to do. I'd go out in the barnyard and bulldog calves or try to ride them like they do in the rodeo. You'd get a pretty good-sized calf and get on it and see how long you could ride before it could throw you off. Sometimes we'd get company and they'd bring kids and we'd have plenty of space to run around.

Some things I'd do over differently. I'd have liked to have been smarter when I moved out of the country school and went to town. The kids there gave me a pretty rough time because I was a farm kid. City kids and farm

Left: Mildred Hammer measuring Young Bill, June 1955.

Above: Young Bill Hammer runs after a flock of sheep.

kids are altogether different. If I had known a little more before I went to town, they wouldn't have given me such a rough time. Scales Mound might not be considered a big town, but at that time it was the main town around here. On Saturday nights you couldn't walk around the aisles in the stores—there was that many people in there. A bunch of us country kids would go in there and buy a watermelon and fill up on it. And we used to have fights with the town kids. We were country kids going into town, and they didn't particularly like it.

Most of the time I spent alone. When I was younger, before I got to riding horses regular with farm neighbor kids, I was mostly alone except for Saturdays and Sundays, when we might have company. I had friends, other kids around the country. But Dad was my best friend.

MILDRED: He was born at my sister's, April 8, 1941. We didn't go to the hospital in those days, you know. That was no serious thing, having a baby, and I went to my sister's and she took care of me. We had a doctor come and I was scared to death of the doctor. He was an old grouch.

Bill was working the morning the doctor was coming to get the baby's name. We had said we were going to name him John. I was lying there in bed and going, "John Hammer, John Hammer—oh heavens, someday they'll call him Jack Hammer. I can't stand that!" So the doctor came and he asked me if I had a name picked and I said we were going to call him John, but I don't like Jack Hammer, and that's what he'd get called. And I said, "I think I'll call him Junior. His dad don't know it, but I think I'm going to call him Junior." The doctor said he'd put that down but to call him if we had to change it. I thought, "That's better than telling him I haven't got a name picked and have him pick my head and tell me, 'You had nine months to pick a name, why don't you have one?'" Bill came that night and I said, "I gave the doctor his name today. You know what I called him?"

He said, "What?"

I said, "Well, it's Hammer, Jr."

I looked at him and he looked at me and he said, "Couldn't you think of a better name than that?"

And I said, "Nope!"

I was real happy that I gave him a son and named him after Bill.

I wanted Junior to grow up in his footsteps—and he did.

Right: Young Bill, September 1959, 18 years old.

BILL AND DOROTHY

Bill, Jr. is eighteen. It is four years since I first photographed Mildred marking his height on the shed door. He was through with school and is working full-time with his father. The truck door now reads "Willis A. Hammer & Son." It was a proud moment for both of them when that addition went on. The farm needed some new things, and Mildred went off to work to help get the cash. But before leaving each morning she would make sure her men had enough food for noontime dinner. The men, as before, spent a lot of time with each other and enjoyed it. Around them the family was growing. Janet had married

Bill Brickner, and they had two little girls. Bill Brickner had grown up in Scales Mound and bought a farm adjoining the Hammers.

Billy started going with Dorothy Hickman. Dorothy lived on a farm a mile out of Scales Mound. The old stagecoach road went by it. Billy never really considered her a farm girl; she lived too close to town, even though her father was a general farmer and her mother worked hard as a farm wife.

DOROTHY: One of the best things was to go after the cows and their calves. There were all these little paths that the cows would make, and we'd have fun trailing those things around, taking a new one each time and watching the way the cows would all follow. I liked the farm up there. It was pretty. In the summer we went walking out in the pastures. It was nice, especially in late afternoon when things would start to cool off. I always enjoyed that, walking around out there. I liked that particular place. It was home.

MILDRED: He had her picture in his billfold and I found it when they were just kids. From the time he started town school, he knew her. They'd go for a while and then they'd decide they were tired of each other and they would go try greener fields.

BILL, JR.: When I first knew Dorothy, or remember knowing her, was when I went to town to grade school. I was in the eighth grade and she was in sixth. Just thought she was a younger grader, didn't even think she was a girl. But then when I was a freshman she was in eighth grade and I dated her, but that was just one date. We didn't hit it off too good. It was my first date. We had to go with a friend of my sister's because they were an older couple. We went to a dance up at school. It was a couple of years before I took her out again.

I didn't ever know for sure if, when I got married, I'd marry a farm girl, but I figured she'd have more in common with me. I started in going with another girl. I still liked Dorothy, but I wasn't about to let her know it for a while. I probably, more or less, took up with this other girl to make Dorothy jealous. I always found that if you chased them they wouldn't have anything to do with you. She got jealous and came after me one night.

Left: Young Bill courts Dorothy at the Cozy Corner Cafe in Scales Mound.

Above: Truck door: "Hammer & Son"

DOROTHY: I always liked his smile. He always had a cute smile. Still does. I knew that someday I was going to marry him before he knew that. When I was a junior, I was queen of our prom. He was going with a girlfriend of mine. I went with another boy. I remember that when I saw him with this girl I just knew that shouldn't be. We'd been going together and then we broke up. We fought a lot. He didn't like me talking to other people but I liked to. He was really jealous. So was I.

I flirted around. I was younger then. I got a friend to tell Bill I wanted him to dance with me. He wouldn't. He was still angry with me. After the prom I went to a girlfriend's house and stayed all night. All we talked about was Bill. I finally woke to the fact that he was the one I wanted to go with. But he started going steady with this other girl. It was May 6. I was in town. So was he, and when I saw him drive out of town I followed him. He went past our place, and I kept on right behind him. He knew something was up. He turned off the blacktop onto his side road. Finally he stopped on down by Brickners' gate. We got out and talked and then we started going together.

I knew that Bill wanted to be a farmer when he was courting me and that I'd be a farmer's wife. It didn't seem bad. I wasn't thinking about that. I was just thinking about being with him.

Above: Scales Mound High School Junior Prom.

Right: Young Bill and Dorothy walk in a field not far from Dorothy's house, followed by her kid brother and a collie.

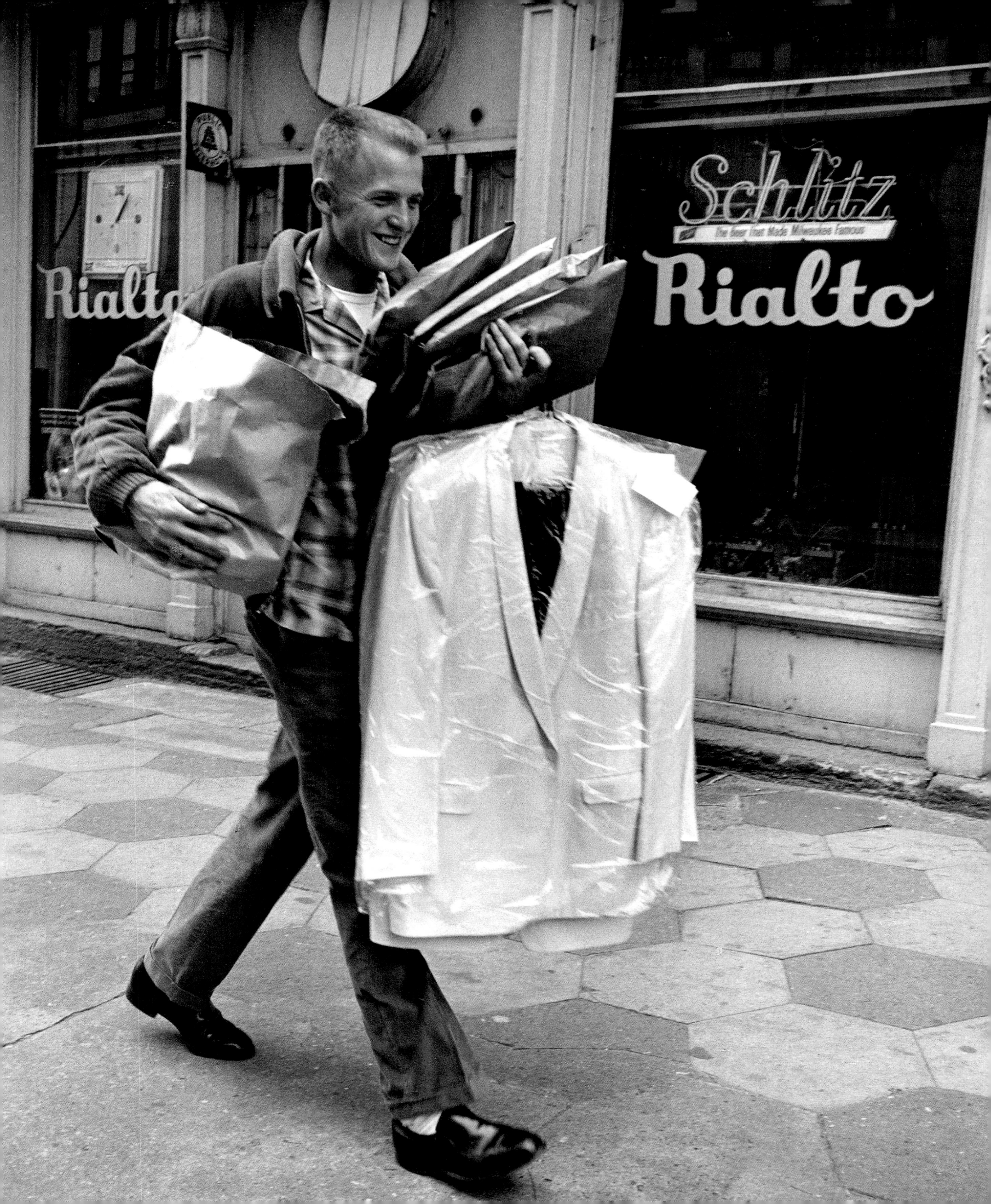
Schlitz
The Beer that Made Milwaukee Famous
Rialto

THE WEDDING

After a three-year courtship, Bill and Dorothy were married in the First Presbyterian Church of Scales Mound. It was May 6, 1961. It was also May 6, a few years before, when Dorothy followed Bill out of town, stopped him at Brickners', and they started going together.

MILDRED: When Junior was getting married, I guess I thought of my own wedding. You listen to the vows and you wonder if you've ever broken any of them. I was very happy about that wedding. He was getting a good girl. She was a girl in the neighborhood and she got a lot of honors in school. I always told her that I was proud of her, that I thought she did great. I bought a graduation present for Dorothy. I wouldn't have done it, the way I did, for anyone else in the world. I was in Aurora and I saw this dress and I said, "That looks like Dorothy!" She wears the same size as Janet. I thought, "Should I buy it for her or shouldn't I?" There was only one of them and I thought, "Yep, I'm going to buy it for her."

I remember the day Dorothy was born. I remember asking Celia what she was going to name her, and I remember her saying, "Dorothy." I saw her grow up. People didn't go out much then, but we were both Presbyterians. Her family belonged to one church and we went to the other. When the two churches would get together, we'd always see them.

Junior and Dorothy had a long-range plan to get married. They didn't rush into it. She graduated high school and went to work, and they were talking about the next year. Then he said, "Well, we've got to start making plans." The summer before they were married he gave her a diamond, so we knew it was coming. He took extra work up at the school to buy her a diamond and, like he said, "It doesn't have to be the biggest in the world, but I don't want them to have to look and look to see it either." On the day he married Dorothy I thought it was the smartest thing he ever did, because I just liked her and thought he made the right choice. I think we are good friends. I hope she thinks we are.

DOROTHY: He never really asked me. We just talked about when we would get married. Setting the date, that took quite a bit of doing. He wanted to get married in April, before the corn planting. I didn't want to before May or June. We finally settled on May, between the oats and the corn.

Marrying Bill was the next step after going together. We went together, we knew we loved each other, we knew we wanted to be together. The next thing, in that day, was to get married; not just go live together. So we got married and on our honeymoon we drove to California. We didn't stay as long as we planned; we came right back here. We do that all the time when we take trips. We can't wait to come back. It's so unreal to be gone. That's the unreal world. When I think about it, it was like a wasting of time. Our real life was back here. We wanted to get back and start living. All I ever thought about being married was that it's going to be great, you're going to be with him all the time.

BILL, JR.: I suppose it would have been nice to have a June wedding. But that's too much of a season for crops, and I can't be running off and getting married. The trip was fantasy—well, it was real, too—but I mean, it just wasn't our life to be traveling around. I mean, it all was new. I was thinking about our future. I was used to my own way. It's quite a change to be married. But I thought she wanted to get married and I loved her and wanted to share my life with her.

Left: Young Bill picking up wedding clothes from the Dubuque rental store.

Above: The wedding party leaves the farmhouse of Bill Brickner, Young Bill's brother-in-law, en route to the wedding at Scales Mound church.

Following pages: After their wedding, Young Bill and Dorothy walk in the same field they had two years before, when they were courting.

41

Left: Young Bill on the day his son, Jim, was
brought home from the hospital.

Above: Dorothy, a month before Jim's birth.

BILL, SR. AND MILDRED

Bill, Sr. and Mildred worked side-by-side to build the farm up and they taught their children their ways, which were honorable and according to the Good Book. They also had grandchildren, Janet's girls. All the family still lived in the valley. They had love for each other and the respect of their neighbors and the profit of twenty-five years of a happy marriage.

To celebrate their anniversary, the Hammers held a reception in Scales Mound at the Flamingo Tea Room, a place built in 1910 as an implement shop. Friends, neighbors, and relatives came with presents and good wishes, and their cars jammed South Railroad Avenue. The talk hummed of the weather, the crops, and memories. It was a day of warm contentment.

BILL, SR.: I was doing chores for my brother, and in between chores I went to town. I met a friend. He didn't have a car and I did; it was a 1930 or '33 Durant. He wanted to know if I wanted to go on a double date that night. I said sure. Mildred was his date. I was taken with her. I don't know if it was that night or at a dance afterwards when I asked her for a date.

MILDRED: Bill was about eighteen. I was sixteen. He was with another boy in Scales Mound. It was Sunday afternoon, and maybe they were playing pool. This boy had a date with me that night, but he didn't have a car. This boy wanted Bill, who had a car, to bring him to see me. They called up and wanted to know if I could get a date for Bill. I got a girl for Bill and I went with my date, and we went to a show in Shullsburg. It was in the wintertime, and a real snowy night. Bill was driving, and we took his date home first, because she lived closer to town than I did. Then, going to my home, we had to go up a big, steep hill called White's Hill, and we couldn't make it up. Bill had to get out and put chains on. He was whistling and working, and this guy I was with was doing nothing but grumbling and grunting, and I just decided, right then and there, that I liked whistling better than I liked groaning and that I liked Bill a lot better than the guy I was dating.

I asked Bill to come to my high-school dance and he took me. We got going together. When he was dating me, he'd use his folks' car sometimes, and sometimes he'd hitch up some horses and he'd take the shortcut under the railroad pass and straight up to my place. We went together for a couple of years, and I was eighteen and he was twenty when we got married.

We were married in the parsonage in Schapville. We had eleven dollars between us. I had six and he had five, so I had controlling interest. It was September 19, 1934, and it was mud. Mud roads, mud everywhere. It was Friday when we were married, and we were back on Monday to go to work. Cutting corn, cutting corn fodder. Cutting it and making shocks, like they used to. In fact, Bill did that in the forenoon and we went and got married in the afternoon. Then we started out for my brother's the first night, because you couldn't stay in any hotels with the kind of money we had. We got going down that hill outside of Scales Mound, and the battery fell out of the car and all over that mud road. Bill just got out, whistled a bit, and put it back in the car.

The first year we came to the homeplace and lived with his folks and brothers. There was enough work, but there were too many people living in one house. One Sunday we took a walk over to the Hesselbachers', and he asked Bill to come and work for him. Bill said, "Well, when do you want me?" We worked for Hesselbacher for eight years.

There were two houses over there, and we had one. But then we wanted to have a farm of our own, be independent. Then one day we were visiting the homeplace here, and Bill's dad was saying that he didn't want to keep the place any longer. He asked the boys if they wanted to buy it, and nobody did but Bill. They said to let Bill buy it, so he did. We moved in here. Grandpa lived with us for a while. Grandma had died while we were over at Hesselbachers'.

Before we got modern and that, I always helped milk. In fact, if the men were out in the field, I could do the chores. I still do field work. Last year I disked 250 acres. Dorothy plowed furrow for furrow with Butch, I disked and harrowed, and Bill planted. That's the way we always went, and I always thought life was good to me.

Left: Bill and Mildred Hammer,
married 25 years.

The Homeplace

The house is more than one hundred years old. Bill, Sr. was born in it. It was his father's house, and he bought it, added to it, raised his children in it. It is called "the homeplace": the place where one belongs and from which every movement is a going away or a coming back.

MILDRED: Bill always wanted this place. I think he grew up with the idea of being here. When I first came here with Bill on dates, he used to talk of having it someday. He loved it. They were working the land with horses then, and he told me he would have black horses and black cattle, and maybe he was kidding when he said black sheep. I suppose he wanted it because the grandfather and the brothers were always here, and his mother and father.

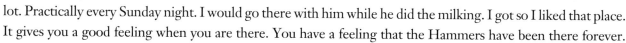

I was wondering a while ago which would ever mean the most to Butch, the homeplace or the one he bought for himself. He told me that this place means more and that he'd lose that place down there before he'd want to lose this one. I understand that. I've got my roots in this house. I'm happy here. But I could build a house on that hill and live up there if it would still be a Hammer that was here.

DOROTHY: In a way, where Bill's folks live is a homeplace to me. I guess probably because it's where Bill used to live. We went there a lot. Practically every Sunday night. I would go there with him while he did the milking. I got so I liked that place. It gives you a good feeling when you are there. You have a feeling that the Hammers have been there forever.

BILL, SR.: It's full of things to remember. I was born and raised here and I know there's something about it here. You kind of dread leaving the house. You wonder whether you'll ever return or not. It's always nice to go, but I'm always interested to get back.

BILL, JR.: Where I live is my home, but the homeplace is at my dad's. Someday, I'll be living there. Maybe it's more or less a habit. Sometimes, before I caught myself, I'd be heading for home and I'd wind up at the homeplace instead of going to where I live. So much of what I am is there. It's just that it's the Hammer place. If things ever got rough, I'd hang on. I'd let everything go before this one because it's the homeplace.

Left: The cross formed on these lace curtains by the window pane reminds one that this is a Christian home.

Above: Bill, Sr.'s brothers and parents. Bill, Sr. is at five o'clock.

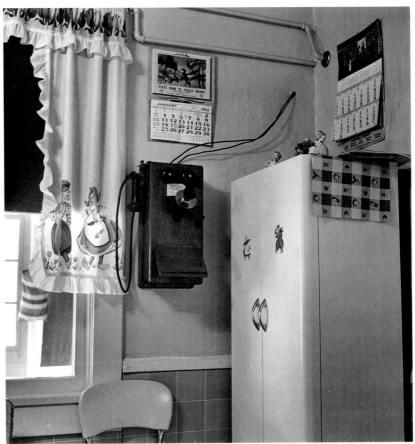

Left: The Hammer barn and silo.

Top: The Hammer homeplace.

Bottom: Corner of the Hammer homeplace kitchen with "farmers' phone," a cooperative neighbors' enterprise.

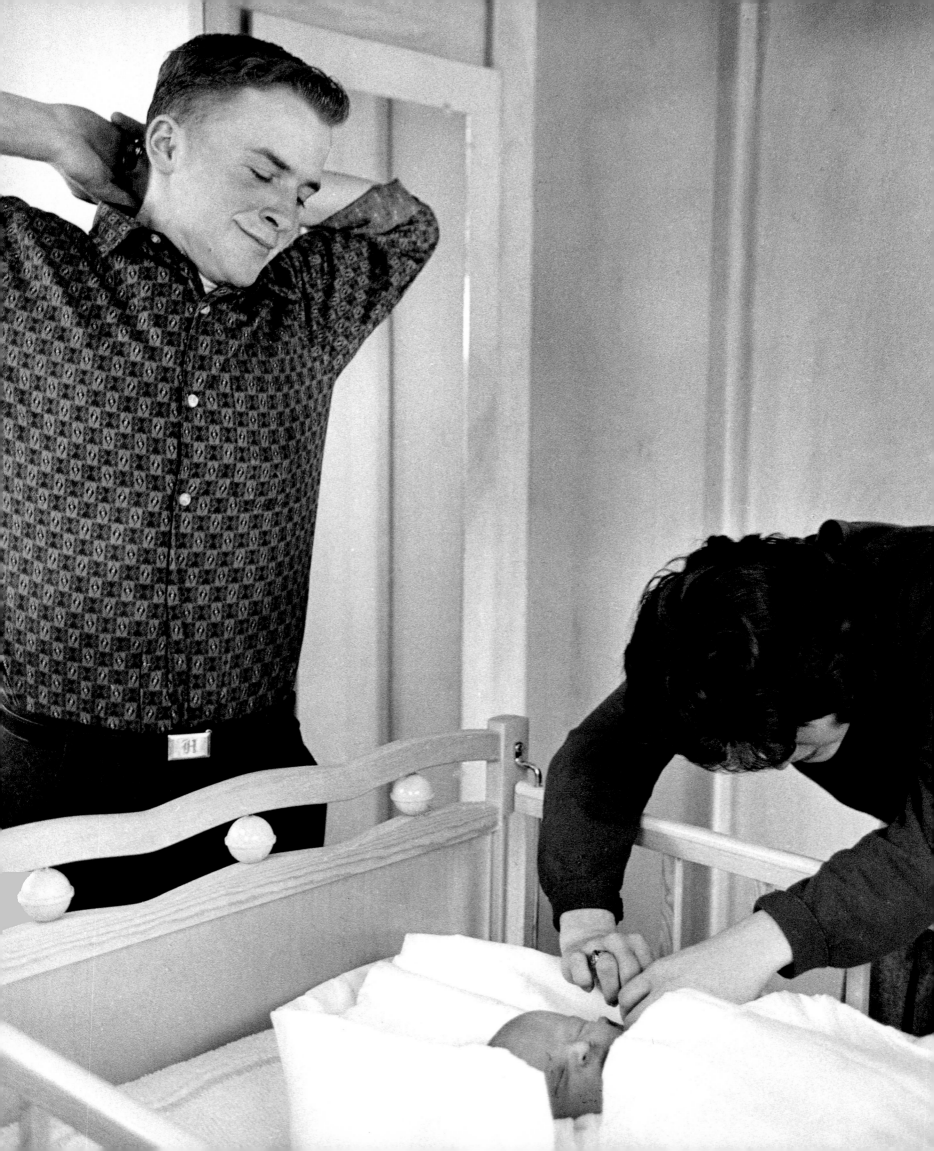

JIM

As Bill, Sr. says, "Rockefellers have heirs. We just have sons." James Alan Hammer was born February 13, 1962. He is the first-born son and grandson in both the Hammer and Hickman families. From the beginning of time that has been special.

DOROTHY: Jim was the first baby I'd really ever seen. When I realized it was mine, I thought "My heavens!" Bill, I guess, was the thrilled one, because he saw him immediately after he was born. I can't remember what he said. I think I was pretty foggy at the time. He probably just smiled a lot—he's very smiley.

It was after midnight. Then he left and went home and I didn't see him until the next night, but he had sent flowers and the card had on it "Thanks for the boy."

BILL, JR.: When I saw Jim for the first time he was in pretty rough shape, but I liked the looks of him. I never liked the looks of babies, but your own you do. I liked him. I was happy.

I was thinking about him being a farmer, same as Dad and me. But I felt the same way as Dad did, and still do, that Jim is going to have to find his own way. If Jim wants to be a farmer, fine! And I'll try to help him, too.

BILL, SR.: I was very happy to think—call it pride, conceit, whatever you want—that there was another Hammer. Well, he's a Hammer. In the immediate family, he's the only Hammer boy to carry on the name.

January 1964. In a month Jim would be two. In 1963, the day after Christmas, his sister Judith was born. The past year was a good year and Dorothy has been busy raising one child and having another. She also baked her own breads and cakes, sewed her own dresses and clothes for her family, worked in her garden, and canned food. Like Mildred, she helped with the men's work: she baled hay, drove the tractor, and cleaned the milking machines. When the men were not eating Mildred's huge noontime dinner at the homeplace, Dorothy enjoyed preparing it at her house. The men never had a weight problem, and the meat, potatoes, creamed corn, string beans, brown gravy, Jell-O salad, bread pudding, fresh butter, hot rolls, jam and honey, fruit drink, milk, coffee, pie, and ice cream suited them well. Janet and Dorothy had combined their efforts in a small, part-time-but-busy sewing business.

Bill and Dorothy had rented the Siskas' land, which adjoined the Hammer fields, and in November they moved their trailer home down there, next to the farmhouse, across the road from the abandoned, weather-beaten, one-room school that Bill had attended and where Ruth Boettner had taught. They had eighteen cows of their own and, along with the landowner's, Bill was milking thirty.

At Thanksgiving 1964, Bill and Dorothy sold the trailer and moved into the Siskas' farmhouse. It had nine rooms, a new bathroom, running water, and a wood-burning furnace. It and 190 acres belonged to the Siskas, a Chicago family. Bill and his father managed it for them. Dorothy took a job. Several days a week she left Jim and Judy with Mildred and drove five miles to a factory located on a 500-acre farm. There she worked an eight-hour shift putting new diamonds and sapphires into old phonograph needles. To Bill and Dorothy, it was only the beginning of what seemed like an endless struggle to keep themselves down on the farm.

Left: Bill and Dorothy Hammer looking at Jim, whom they have just brought home after his birth. Bill stretches with pride and good feeling.

Above: Jim Hammer at age two and a half.

A TIME FOR THANKS

In 1966 Bill and Dorothy bought a small farm next to the village where the elder Hammers were married. In a letter dated "Schapville, U.S.A., June 17, 1966," Dorothy wrote: "Things seem to be going along pretty good for the entire Hammer family. Thank God. The kids love it here and they are growing like crazy. Bill and his dad have the corn all in and are getting ready for the haying season. They are making plans for a new milking parlor, milk house with a large bulk tank and all, and a giant pole shed or loafing shed for the cows. Since we have combined the herds, the milk checks are getting bigger and bigger."

By March 1967, the new milking parlor was complete. The father-son partnership flourished. Dorothy was pregnant with her third child, Jayne. When they sat down to supper at Young Bill's house and said grace, it seemed like a special time for thanks. On Sundays or when the whole family was together, they always said grace. "Thank you for the food which we are about to receive and the blessings which you have bestowed upon us through Jesus Christ our Lord, Amen."

DOROTHY: You're always saying thanks to God, but not always in words. It's more a feeling of thankfulness. Like supper: The day is over, the work is done for the day, and you have a feeling of thanks for the food you have, for the day, and for having children. You're thankful for God's favors.

BILL, JR.: You don't ask Him for favors.

MILDRED: There are a lot of people in the grave would take what I have, gladly. There's that story about the farmer that rejuvenated this plot of ground that hadn't been worth anything, and he had a beautiful crop on it. The minister came along and told him he had so much there to thank God for, and he said to the minister, "Yeah, but you ought to've seen it when it was just God's alone."

BILL, SR.: Naturally, there's always a mystery to how things happen when you're farming. You take it for granted and you're thankful that they happen as they do. We live with it. We're thankful, but we don't think about it.

MILDRED: It gets to be like breathing.

Left: Sunday dinner with the Hammer family
at Bill and Dorothy's Schapville farmhouse.

Following pages: Bill Hammer, Jr. in the
doorway of the milking parlor.

The Women

There is a lilt to it when the women say, "The men are out in the field," or the men say, "The women are in the kitchen." There is men's work and there is women's work.

MILDRED: I think it goes back to the Bible. It's a religious understanding. That's the way the work gets divided: This chore's yours and that chore's mine.

Maybe it's just old-time talk. There was one farmer around here that when he wanted his wife he'd holler, "Hey, woman!" Even our hired hand, when he wanted me, instead of calling me by name, he'd stand out in the yard and holler, "Hey, woman!"

I'd rather do women's work than men's work. I'd rather cook, do the gardening and yard work, raise chickens, and help out wherever I see a place to do things and knowing how to do them. Being a good helpmate is not having to do it, but being able to do it, if he's sick or if he's not here. I help in the field and I scrub the milk house and polish it from one end to the other. I guess there's where women's work and men's work comes in.

I'd like to stay on the farm when I retire. I guess if you fall in love with a man, and you get married to him, it's mostly being with him and helping him that counts. When I was a teenager I never did think about what I was going to do. It didn't matter until Bill came along. I've always been glad that I was with Bill. I've always felt needed.

There were those years when I worked away from home. I was working to improve the standard of living. We needed cash. Junior was getting into cars, Janet was getting married, and we needed some new machinery. I was awful glad the day I could quit and come home to stay.

I enjoyed the whole thing of my life, the work and the kids, the way it went. I think every man wants a son and every woman does, too. We got both kinds that we wanted, a son and a daughter. My relationship with Junior was come and go; he was his dad's. In the high moments of his life I always knew Junior liked me more than he let on. You'd hear him bragging how Mom made this and how Mom made that and he'd go to a picnic and tell them, "That's my mom's potato salad." He had an aversion to being called a sissy. When he was about ten years old he said, "Now you stop calling me Billy; you make me sound like a sissy when you call me Billy. You call me Butch. It makes me sound tough."

I was born in Wisconsin—just across the line—on a farm. Mom didn't dance, so I was Dad's square-dancing partner. We danced at neighborhood parties. Oh, how I loved that, dancing with Dad.

DOROTHY: I learned a lot from Millie. She always made me feel at home. When I went there I always took part and it makes you feel like you're one of them. On a farm, the woman's the helping hand and a partner. But I'd rather be the woman than the man. I couldn't take some of the pressure that he takes. I worry about it, yes, but I always figure he'll take care of it. I mean, he always does.

BILL, JR.: There's women's work and there's men's work. She should just get along with him, be backing him instead of fighting him, and have respect for him. If your wife loses respect for you, you're in trouble. And the man's work is making a good enough living to keep your wife respecting you.

Left: Dorothy and Mildred Hammer

DOROTHY

Dorothy's mother was from Benton, Wisconsin. Dorothy's father is from Scales Mound, where she grew up on the family farm. Even with farm chores Dorothy thinks that being a farm wife is the same as being a mother and wife anywhere. Once, working with Old Bill—she disked and he planted—a neighbor admired her work. Old Bill told him, "Now you know why I am so proud of Dorothy."

DOROTHY: When they need me to do something, I have to be willing to do it. Besides, I enjoy being out on a tractor, and around here I don't see Bill that often during the day unless I'm working with him. Sometimes it's nine o'clock at night before I get to see him. I like being a farm wife. I mean, I like being away from people, being by myself with Bill and the kids. Bill's folks live the way I like to live. At the homeplace you can look out and you can see your neighbors, but they're far enough away that you're not breathing down each other's throat. You can look out and say, "Oh, there's Carl out there today, making hay."

I look forward to my children grown up. Well, it's like you're writing chapters and waiting to see how it ends. It's a story. It'll be a good story, I think.

I think that I'd like to see Bill have more. Like the new tractor. I was thrilled for him, because it was what he wanted for a long time. And then I think we'd like having a real nice place. Not that we have to have all new because you can make an old place look nice if you try. It's like this area. It's old and you know most everybody. It's a nice feeling. Especially if you come from a good family. People say, "Well, you're a Hickman," or "You're a Hammer. I know your dad and grandpa." Having roots is a good thing.

Left: Dorothy Hammer discing on a tractor.

Grandma Schultz in front of her Schapville house.

Christmas angels in the Schapville Zion Presbyterian Church.

Jayne Hammer and Bettye Brickner

Jayne Hammer and Bettye Brickner at their graduation from Scales Mound High School.

Old Bill Hammer's Aunt Emma Hammer

Pastor Donna, Schapville Presbyterian Church.

Baby shower for Dorothy Hammer.

Pastor Donna

Clockwise from left: Voting workers Marie Eversoll, Myrtle Stadel, Betty Roberts, Esther Lieberman, Margaret Stevens.

Tammy Stadel (Chrystal's daughter)

Chrystal Stadel

Marie Eversoll

Chrystal Stadel in truck.

Joyce, Jayne, and Leah Grube (Meldon and Evelyn's daughters)

Evelyn Grube

Judy Hammer

The Sewing Bee

June 8, 1987. Marie Eversoll's kitchen.

MARIE EVERSOLL: Church is changing entirely, like our women's group, which has been quilting since 1920 and has almost run out. We only have from four to six, at the most. We still have a sewing circle, it's small but they don't seem to want to give it up, completely.

January 3, 1973. Marie Eversoll's parlor. The quilters are Betty Rogers, Myrtle Rury, Dorothy Dittmer, Annelle Rury, Meta Stadel, Mildred Hammer, Marie Eversoll, and Olga Dittmer, and they are gathered around a quilting frame. When they speak at the same time it's hard to tell whose voice is the one being heard.

MARIE: We do this once a month on Thursday—the first Thursday of the month. We've been doing it since 1920— that's fifty-three years, isn't it? Not all of us have been doing it since 1920, though.

MILDRED: It's not hard to quilt, but I don't know where I'm going. Like driving down the road behind a gas truck.

VOICE: Where does this go from here, now?

VOICE: Should you move through here, too?

VOICE: Can you do some of that there, I'm going over this way.

VOICE: There goes the coo-coo clock.

MARIE: I know, when it's not running the whole house feels sad.

VOICE: How come Curly didn't want that clock that Paul had?

MARIE: This one isn't as shrill, I think is why.

VOICE: He don't hear it upstairs, either?

MARIE: Well, in the summertime I can hear the coo-coo outside if I have the doors open. 'Cause I work out in the garden and when it coo-coos eleven I know it's time for me to stop and clean off my hoe and come in. It carries quite far. And we can hear it upstairs, too. But it don't keep us awake or anything.

VOICE: Here's something in this magazine: "Housewives can be beautiful."

MARIE: That's a good title for it anyway. Janet is beautiful and she's still got the wonderful figure that she always had.

MILDRED: That time that guy drove in. She was outside working. He wanted to know if she still got her dress. And could she still get into it.

Preceding pages: Sewing bee. *Clockwise from left:*
Marie Eversoll, Myrtle Rury, Dorothy Dittmar,
Annelle Rury (Myrtle's daughter-in-law), Meta
Stadel (Marvin's wife and George's mother),
Mildred Hammer, and Olga Dittmar (Marie's sister)

MARIE: I guess I don't have to worry about the dinner drying on our plates. I can just put them in the wastepaper basket. The casseroles were awful good. The green beans. I really enjoyed it.

VOICE: The boys don't care for green beans.

MARIE: I'll tell you. Something that you make up in a hurry is much more tasty than something that you fuss over.

META: Well those beans is easy to make. You just dump your beans in your casserole and your mushroom soup. Marvin likes onion rings on top.

ANNELLE: I don't care too much for onions.

META: Who was it said they saw Marvin go down?

MARIE: I know that when I was out there fussing around I saw him go by.

META: Probably ate downtown. Tired of the old lady's cooking.

VOICE: If he's tired of my cooking he can cook his own.

META: Well, I don't think Marvin is much of an expert. He's pretty hard on the cheese and the eggs.

VOICE: You have quite a bit of chickens.

META: No. They just quit laying.

VOICE: I have the kind of hens that lay every three or four days.

VOICE: They're going to quit.

VOICE: No, they just got started.

ANNELLE: Like that man who was trying to find somebody that would have an old hen that would sit on some pheasant eggs. She said they don't sit anymore.

MILDRED: Maybe they're liberated.

All laugh.

VOICE: We had one that sat and hatched a baby pigeon.

MILDRED: I read in the magazine the other day of a woman that set turkey eggs in an electric blanket. She hatched turkey eggs in the blanket.

VOICE: We don't use electric blankets anymore, we use comforters.

VOICE: I use comforters but I can't get warm.

THE MEN

They are called Old Bill and Young Bill.

BILL, JR.: "Never take out anybody you wouldn't want to marry." That was the main thing Dad told me, the one I remembered the most. Most of what he taught me he didn't say in words; it was through work and doing. He didn't say "Don't do this" or "Don't do that." He let me experiment a little. I'd just watch him to see how he did it, and some things I'd try to do the same way and added my own touch to it.

As far as going out and playing games—baseball, or going fishing, or anything like that—we never did. It was the routine of doing the work and going along. Why, I'd be so proud if I got so I could load some bales, help him out! Then the next year I'd be that much older and then I could load half the load, and pretty quick I was loading the whole works!

BILL, SR.: That was when I liked it!

BILL, JR.: Each year, he'd give me more responsibility. If I'd do something wrong, he'd just tell me, "Well, do it the other way." He never did cuss much. If he ever cussed, you knew it was pretty bad.

BILL, SR.: I never could see getting all stewed up about something. I've seen the time when something'd happen and Junior would say, "Well, aren't you going to swear?" Well, no. What for? It wouldn't do any good. I had a good relationship with my father even though I had three brothers. It was about the same as Junior and me.

BILL, JR.: I think your father was tougher on you than you were on me. If he said "Do it this way," you better do it that way. He was really the head of the household.

BILL, SR.: That generation was more headstrong.

BILL, JR.: We've made changes. Like being partners. We own things together, and that allows us to make good use of the machines we own. Here's where our relationship has always been pretty good: One guy doesn't expect the other guy to do more than the first one does. If he milks five nights a week, he doesn't begrudge it if I'm not milking, and I don't begrudge it that he isn't milking when I am. If we go out to drive stakes and I drive fifty steel stakes and he doesn't, well, fine! I don't feel that I'm doing more than he. We're both working for the same thing. When there's something to be done, we both do it. Neither of us will leave the other alone.

BILL, SR.: I was paying a lady in a store in town when Butch came in, and she said, "I see you have the boss with you today again." I said, "Well, I very seldom go very far without him," and she said, "You know, that's what I always liked and admired about you two. You get along so well, you're always together, and you're always working together." It's a good feeling when you hear things like that.

JIM HAMMER, (age 10): I know what it takes to be a farmer. He's a man who's strong, a man who can think, make decisions quick, and all that. A man like my dad.

Left: Bill, Sr., Bill, Jr. and Jim Hammer

Above: Jim's name added to the truck door.

Following pages: Bill, Sr., Bill, Jr. and Jim Hammer in field with tractor. The picture (without Jim) that gave me the idea for this project in 1955 has now come full circle.

Pages 74-75: Bill Hammer, Jr. and his son, Jim, are framed by the barn door while they wait for hay.

Bill Hammer, Sr. and grandson Jim.

Larry Werner and son Justin.

Repainting the feed store building in Scales Mound.

Hunter's trunk at Curly Eversoll's.

Dorothy Hammer measuring Jim.

Margarite Eversoll with Reverend Dexter.

County Fair building in Warren, Illinois.

Carl Grube (Meldon's son)

Ernie Boettner

Jay Dexter and pet duck.

Jay Dexter as a young man.

Henry Hoppe with his minister, Reverend Dexter.

Norm Winslow of Scales Mound.

Schapville Road sign with bullet holes.

Eddie Saam chewing tobacco.

Sarge Stegall's house in Schapville, where Ricky grew up.

Joel Dexter is the second of four sons of Reverend John Paul Dexter and his wife, Shirley.
He and his three brothers, Jeff, Josh, and Jay, plus Ricky Stegall, Kenneth and David
(they called him Smiley because his two front teeth were missing) Knauer, Dean Williams
(Henry Hoppe's grandson), the Winter and the Stadel boys made up their group.

Joel says there weren't any girls in town when he was growing up except for Tammy
Stadel and she was too young. And other girls were "too far."

JOEL DEXTER

Joel's family moved to Schapville when he was a child and he remained after his family left. He lived in an abandoned log cabin, the Schwartz place, Ernie Boettner's grandfather's place, where the drinking water froze on bitter cold nights. He drove a truck without a starter and took advantage of the hills to start it. Eventually, he left Schapville, but he returns every year to strengthen his memories. Now it is May 1987, and Joel remembers.

JOEL: I worked with Georgie (the road commissioner) on the roads. They called me "The Holy Roller," maybe because my dad was the Lutheran minister and because I rolled the tractor over three times one summer. George said, "You're supposed to mow the ditches from fence to fence," which is really impossible, but I tried my best. And lucky to be alive, too. I had a roll cage and a seat belt, too. I hung upside down in that roll cage a couple times. (*He laughs.*)

Now Joel is looking at photographs.

JOEL: There's my folks' anniversary and that was before my dad's accident. That kind of changed his appearance. There's my dad with a mustache. He looked good with a mustache. There's my dog, Don Juan. Had to shoot him, he got hit by a car. We had dogs named Honeycomb, Sesser, Calamity Jane.

Here's one. This is the first time my dad came back to church after the accident. See that one eye. He was real dizzy. We had to help him up to the pulpit. We were helping out with the sermon. He was very popular, my

dad was, around here. When he had the motorcycle accident one of his congregation stopped and the guy didn't know it was my dad—his clothes were all ripped off and he was all bloody. He was lucky to get out alive.

We were all kind of rebellious. When I got to be a teenager, for a while, I used to go to the Presbyterian church. I thought it was a real warm church. I rebelled against my dad and his church.

There's my old car— you know it's still over in Galena. I'm on my eighth car now.

I think about my old truck. That old truck didn't have a starter so I could only visit people on top of hills. One time I was in Galena and I parked on a hill. I got it so I could start in reverse. Roll backwards and pop the clutch into reverse and get started.

That's Ricky on the back of my motorcycle.

Ricky Stegall was a neighbor and after school I went up to Ricky's a lot of times. His father, Sarge, was usually in town. Ricky had a little BB pistol and we could shoot darts with it. Rick had a rat that would come out of his hole in the wall. Rick had a dart in his BB gun and he tied a string to it, because he was afraid that if he shot the rat it would crawl back into its hole. So he tied a string to the dart and he shot the rat right in the head. The rat ran to his hole and Ricky pulled it out.

Then there was Dean Williams, Henry Hoppe's grandson. One time we stole a six-pack of beer from Henry Hoppe. We didn't even want to drink it. We had to force down two bottles, then we had our guns and we shot the other bottles. We got in a lot of trouble for that from Henry Hoppe. He didn't talk to me at all but he talked to Dean quite a bit!

Page 76: The Dexter family. *From left:* Shirley and Reverend John Paul Dexter, sons Jeff, Joel, Jay, and Josh.

Left: Joel Dexter on motorcycle with Ricky Stegall behind him.

Above: Reverend Dexter's first service after his accident.

Grandma Mary Schultz

JOEL: Grandma Schultz she always told us to call her Grandma when we moved to Schapville. Every time we would ride our horses by she would come out and say, "When are you going to give me a ride?" And she'd call them ponies, "When are you going to give me a ride on your ponies?"

She was actually Rick Stegall's grandma. And he always said, "How come you call her Grandma?"

I would say, "She told us to."

He would say, "She's not your grandma, she's my grandma."

She was one of the nicest ladies. I always loved to talk to her. She never had running water in that house. Never did. She used to get water from Sarge's pump, called the town pump. It was really sad because she had lived ninety-five years and she was completely different. She just quit eating and she cried a lot and she just said, "Leave me alone. I want to die." She had always been a happy person.

Henry Hoppe's Father

JOEL: Henry told me stories about his dad in the Civil War. They were riding along once, and one of the troops found a snake in his saddle. It was what he called a "hoop snake." The snake bit onto his own tail, rolled up into a hoop, followed that soldier and got up under his saddle. The soldier bit the snake and it died. That was kind of a corny story.

Jack Eversoll

JOEL: Curly's dad, Jack Eversoll. He's famous. The hill he lived on was infested with rattlesnakes. He would catch bunches of them. They say he used to lead them around with a shoe string. He used to catch them and put them in these grain bags. He had an old Model A, with a toolbox on the fender. He'd carry the snakes around in that toolbox so people wouldn't steal the tools out of his toolbox. In Elizabeth someone asked him what was in the sack.

He said, "A rattlesnake."

And the guy said, "No it's not either." And he reached for the sack and it just started to rattle. Then he believed old Jack.

Jack Eversoll, he's the only guy in town with an all-glass storm door on his outhouse. So he has an excellent view.

Ernie Boettner

JOEL: Ernie! I looked up to him ever since I was a little kid. He was always so calm and he'd come in and visit us, sit there in my dad's chair and smoke his pipe and hardly say a word. Pretty soon he was gone and you wondered, "Where did Ernie go?" He would appear and disappear. With hardly a word.

I always wondered what made Ernie so contented. He said he wasn't, though. He said he was restless. I can believe that. He's hard to keep up with. I helped him clear out a fence line hottest day of the year. He was out there running a chain saw and cutting cedar trees down. It was exhausting for me. He could climb over a fence quicker than I could. He's strong as an ox. He was around eighty years old then.

Curly Eversoll

JOEL: We used to pester him all the time. Not on purpose but just to go to him at the garage and talk to him, ask him questions. Just to be around him. And I suppose we got in his way.

When we first moved to Schapville we used to make prank phone calls and my oldest brother, Jeff, got the bright idea of calling Curly and saying (trying for a deep authoritative voice), "Hello. You Curly?"

He'd answer and say, "Yes I am."

Jeff would say, "Well, straighten up!"

I don't know if Curly knew who did it. He's kind of an institution around here.

Curly and Marie, they still live here. They always will.

Right: Ricky Stegall, Joel Dexter, and David "Smiley" Knauer

RICKY STEGALL

Ricky Stegall's father married into Schapville when he married Grandma Schultz's daughter. People remember that when Ricky was a boy growing up and hunting around Schapville, he shot a rabbit and gave it to a neighbor for Christmas. It is remembered as a generous gift.

RICKY: Grandma lives in the little house between the garage and our house. With the trees in front. Grandpa owned our house. He died before I was born. So I don't know nothing about him except he had a lot of gray hair. I know from pictures. Grandma's name is Mary Schultz. Mary Jane Schultz.

Relatives are Red Schultz in Scales Mound, Ernie Schultz in Freeport. Red is her son, I'm pretty sure. My mother was Red's sister. See, when I was in fourth grade that's when she died. I was eight when she died. I don't know where Grandma came from. She's home all the time. You don't call her Mary, or something, just call her Grandma, everyone else does.

I can't find anything to do at night. It's always like this. Everybody is watching TV and I don't like watching TV all the time. I'm bored at Schapville so I have to go out and hunt. Whatever is in season. Rabbit, coon, squirrel, that's all I hunt. Then there is pheasant. I don't know what else. I just hunt the rabbit and the squirrel and the coon. I started using guns about a year or so ago. I'm fifteen. November 2, 1958.

My dad is a retired captain. He's a demolition expert. In the army. He just sits at home with his television. He's from Latoga, that's around Galesburg. For a while he was a cop at the ordnance depot, and he put some rockets together up there and then he was a demolition expert. When he got out of the army he was a cop up there. He was in the service for twenty years, he retired before I was born. I never knew him as an army captain. He used to live up in Scales Mound, though he moved up here when I was born. I don't think I ever asked him where he met my mother. No, I never asked him. I can't even think where she came from. I don't know nothing about my family. I just never asked. I never really needed to know.

Marie Eversoll is related to the Grebners, Dittmers, and Winters. Curly Eversoll is also related to the Winters, but Marie makes it clear that it is to a "different kind of Winter." Curly is also related to Anton Schap.

Curly was born in Schapville, and he and Marie have lived all their married life here. Curly ran a garage, fixed cars and tractors and anything else that had a motor. He keeps honeybees and bottles honey for sale. He sells and services chain saws and won an award for selling an amazing number of them in this out-of-the-way place.

Everybody knows Curly.

THE EVERSOLLS
CURLY AND MARIE

THE EVERSOLLS

A December Saturday: The Eversoll house looks out on new shapes the snow has made of the trees, the hills, the cemetery, and its gravestones. The wood stove in Marie's kitchen warms the house, and breakfast is sweetened with the smell of wood smoke and honey, the summer's wages from Curly's beehives. Curly's eleven-year-old grandson, Greg, wants to leave this comfort to see if Curly's traps caught raccoons. But Greg waits as Curly talks about Anton Schap.

CURLY: Anton Schap was married to a sister of my grandmother. That was right after the Civil War. When he got back from the Civil War was when he built the blacksmith shop and started his wagon factory and settled here. I'll tell you he was an artist. He was an artist with wood or iron. It was just too bad that he couldn't stay away from booze.

In the wintertime when the Mississippi froze over he would take a team of horses on the river and go to Dubuque which is thirty miles away and then he'd go on a big drunk over there, put his team in a livery stable, I guess. He would be drunk for a few days and then he'd sober up and get a big load of wagon wood, bolsters and reaches and everything like that, and then he would bring the "sloade up the shood," so to put, and go all the way down the Mississippi on the ice. All the way down to where the Galena River runs into the Mississippi, up the Galena River to Galena and then home. He maybe divided his load when he got to Galena because his team wouldn't

pull it up these hills. Probably made two trips to Galena then. I would imagine it would have taken a full day to get to Dubuque. But he maybe had a team that moved right along. And on the ice, once you got that team moving, the horses could trot. That was the only flat place around here, and all the way up the Galena River you could call it level. Practically level, almost level. That's the way he got his yearly supply of wood for building wagons. Oh, he was a smart fellow.

On my dad's dad's side there was a mercenary who came to fight in the Revolutionary War. My dad's mother came from Germany. The Eversolls themselves have been in this country for years and years. My grandfather Eversoll was born here. My grandfather and grandmother Winter, on my mother's side, both came from Germany about 1850 when the Germans came. My grandmother Winter was a baby when she came across and she got sick on the boat and they had her all wrapped up and ready to throw her overboard as dead when another lady on the

Page 84: Marie and Curly Eversoll at their 50th wedding anniversary celebration in the Schapville Zion Presbyterian Church.

Left: The Eversolls' kitchen door. The church is in the background.

Above: Curly and Marie Eversoll

boat said, "That baby isn't dead yet," and she did revive and lived to be quite old. And then the Elizabeth who was surrounded by the Blackhawks, the woman who was credited with saving the fort, was one of my relatives.

That would have been Elizabeth Winter, one of the three famous Elizabeths who were inside Apple River Fort when it was surrounded by Indians in the summer of 1832. The women (and their children) loaded guns for the men so quickly and the men were able to fire so rapidly that the Indians were fooled into thinking they faced a larger force. After three-quarters of an hour the Indians withdrew, having killed only one man.

CURLY: I was born in 1914. I had a sister named Myrtle. I got my name Carlyle because that was my dad's idea. Where he ever heard the name I don't know. He named all his boys with a C. There was Colin, Cletus, and Clifford. One boy died at two days old, his name was Carson.

It is not uncommon. Reverend Dexter's kids' names start with Js, the Brickners' with Bs, and the George Stadels' with Ds.

CURLY: When I started to grade school in Schapville it was a two-room schoolhouse. Then they closed the lower room after the first year I went to school there. In the one room, at one time, we had forty-seven kids and eight grades. Then I went to high school in Stockton. I had an aunt and uncle that lived on a little farm on the east edge of Stockton and I had a chance to work for my board and room. And I was mighty happy that I had that privilege. I finished high school— you bet I did!

MARIE: I went to Thompson Center, where the Apple Canyon Lake now is.

CURLY: That's when those timber wolves were still there.

The only business in Schapville at one time was Curly's garage.

CURLY: I built the garage in '46. Delmar Dittmar and I just about died from carbon monoxide. It was in the middle of winter. It was a real cold day. There was a lot of cars that wouldn't start and they'd tow them to my shop and we'd push them in and I'd put the battery charger on them and get them started and run them a minute or two and back them out and get another one in. That went on and on before noon. Wasn't used to a tight building. Then Delmar Dittmar came with his Model A and needed the brakes adjusted. I remember working on the brake rods and adjusting the brakes and I suppose I was barely moving.

MARIE: I called because it was twelve-thirty and you weren't home yet.

CURLY: Well, we lost track of time and I probably wasn't getting much accomplished either. So we walked back to the house and coming up the hill I said to Delmar, "This is below zero weather. I believe I'll go sit down awhile." He said, "You'll freeze to death. We'd better keep on going." So we got on over to the house, and, of course, Marie had a good dinner fixed for us. I wasn't in any mood to eat, but I ate a piece of pumpkin pie. I remember that and I went back over to the shop. I was trying to put in points and I was leaning over and I thought my head was going to split and I would have to go out the side door and heave. Roy Winter was there and said, "I believe you ought to be home in bed." That's all it took. I finished putting in those points and I came home. I thought I was going to die. And did my head ache! I was a week getting over that.

Curly says to his grandson, "Well, come on, Greg, let's go. It's time to check the traps."

Curly's family, like him, never owned a lot of land. Curly's house is on a half acre. Curly hunts on others' land. No one minds.

CURLY: This is a real beautiful morning. I had a pair of dandy coons last evening. Oh! We forgot to set that one trap. Didn't you, Greg?

Greg has been watching, listening and emulating his grandpa's walk. They have walked a long way. Curly stops. The squeak and crunch of boots in the snow stops.

CURLY: Now here's one set. I know where all the dens are and I just set the traps in the dens. It comes from years of hunting around here. There's lots of coon around here, too many. That's why I'm trapping, to keep the population down a little so they don't get sick and probably all die.

Later, inside Marie's kitchen, Curly makes coffee for himself and hot cocoa for Greg.

CURLY: It's going to taste a lot better than it did early this morning.

Curly lights up a cigarette, one that he rolled himself.

CURLY: I call them camels because each one has a hump on them.

Curly has these stories.

CURLY: Did I ever tell you about my old hunting and trapping partner that got killed one time? Well, he was a great guy to be always looking at tracks and one day he was walking across this field and he saw a set of tracks and he stooped down to examine the tracks and the train came along and run over him and killed him. Ha, ha. Did you get that, Greg?

Marie has heard the story before.

MARIE: Greg is pretty lucky to have a granddad like Curly and smart as him. Curly's pretty smart. He hunts and does mechanics and all kinds of things. But if you think he's smart you ought to have met his dad.

CURLY: Oh, he was smart. And he could invent things. He invented a fly-powered circus. It takes a pretty good size fly. Not just a plain housefly. It takes a little bigger fly than that. He'd take a pin and stick it through the tail of a fly and stick that in a board. Then he'd take a cork and put a pin through that and stick that in the board just under the fly's legs. The fly would try to get away and its legs would spin the cork.

Here's another one. You have to have your equipment ready and that is a pin stuck through a piece of paste board or something so the pin stands up straight. Then you take a light pin or a needle and take two little chunks of cork and stick one of these pieces on each end of the needle. Then you catch a fly and you stick its tail first onto the pin that's mounted in the cardboard. Then you take the needle with the corks on the ends—it looks like a dumbbell—and you hand that to the fly and he will just keep working that back and forth. He's trying to get off the pin so he's just working this dumbbell. I used to do that in school. I'd have one setting on my desk.

Above: Curly Eversoll and grandson Greg Frank bring in a raccoon they have trapped.

Right: Curly Eversoll's raccoon pelts. They are hanging on "supers" used in beekeeping.

Curly remembers farmer Will Wasmund.

CURLY: He used to drive a team of horses into Scales Mound. He could stand a lot of cold on his hands. He was an old German. They had about five kids. Will Wasmund was superstitious. He claimed the reason his wife died was because they took her to the hospital on a Friday.

MARIE: There were bad things could happen. There was this William Hammer—he'd be a cousin to Albert and some sort of relative to old Bill Hammer, Millie's husband. This William Hammer's father committed suicide when they had a flood and it washed out all his corn.

CURLY: Then William Hammer had both his barns burned down when lightning hit them.

MARIE: The same night.

Marie and Curly are talking about their marriage.

MARIE: He courted me for four years.

CURLY: Oh well, I knew her as soon as I knew anybody. We went to Sunday school together. And my mother and

Marie's mother went to Ladies' Aid. Before we started grade school we were always together. We knew one another a long time. We went to the Sunday school right across the road. But being she's older than I am, why, she probably knew me longer than I knew her.

MARIE (laughing): Just a few months older.

And then, all of a sudden, it was 1938 and we went to Nashua, Iowa, to be married in the Little Brown Church in the Vale. Lots of people do that, they go to Nashua to be married. It's a long way. It must be two or three hundred miles. We took our minister along. Like I say, it isn't the church building that makes it that important. Reverend Tjaden was our minister. He thought it was a great idea. I guess you could say our minister went on our honeymoon with us.

But we didn't stay there in Nashua, we came right back. It was evening when we got back and Marie's mother had a big supper for the minister, my dad and mother, one aunt and uncle, my brothers and sister. We had a house full of people at supper. Marie's foster brother and the minister's wife went with us to Nashua. It was November 23.

Tell about the shivaree.

CURLY: Then after supper the whole countryside came and shivareed us. At Marie's folks' place in Thompson Center. We had two barrels of beer and a double header. And all the cheese and crackers they could eat. It was just like any shivaree. They had old buzz saws and disc blades, anything that made a lot of noise, you know. And I suppose a few shot guns, and fire crackers, and anything that made noise. And did they make noise! Oh, there was a houseful of people.

MARIE: Seventy seven people.

CURLY: And then they'd take up a collection and that usually pays for the beer and cheese and crackers.

MARIE: Instead of having a shower, everybody that came to shivaree brought gifts.

CURLY: They didn't have showers in those days.

Above: Announcement box outside the church.

Right: Marie and Curly Eversoll, surrounded by neighbors, friends, and family on their 50th wedding anniversary at Schapville Zion Presbyterian Church.

Following pages: Curly Eversoll at his anniversary, putting on the hat he wore when he and Marie were married 50 years before.

MARIE: Where the Grauses live was built in the 1920s by Conrad Bahr and there's where Louise Bahr—we called her Lolie—worked as the central telephone operator. That was our own company; we had our own community company. We'd call it the farmers' telephone. This is where the last telephone was, which was operated by Lolie until 1966. The Schapville Telephone Company was started in 1906. It had its own laws, that in the wintertime you could just call central from 7 A.M. until 8 P.M. In the summertime you could call from to 6 A.M. to 9 P.M. On Sunday you could just call between 7 and 8 in the morning and from 7 to 8 in the evening. It cost $4 a year when it started and $12 a year when it closed.

CURLY: The farmers had to come together to fix their own lines and they had to build their own lines, too. We didn't have any numbers. You'd ask Lolie to plug you into whoever you wanted to talk to. Somebody from the outside might use numbers, you'd call and Lolie would get on the line and you'd say, "I want to talk to so and so, number is Ring 3."

If I'd go to Dubuque after parts, say in the spring when it was a real busy time, before I left I'd call Lolie and I'd say, "Well, I'm going to Dubuque. If anyone calls tell them where I'm at." So when I got back I'd call Lolie, "Did anyone want me this afternoon?"

She'd tell me, "Oh yes. Willis Hammer is having tractor trouble. Wants you to call him."

That telephone kept this community together more than anything else. More than the churches or anything. Really, it did. Lolie could give a general ring if there was a fire or somebody was in big trouble. All she'd have to do is give a general ring and the whole community, probably, twenty-five or thirty different families all at the same time and in a few minutes, knew it. You could get a group of people together in a twinkling if someone needed help. I'll tell you, that was when the community started to go to pot when our old telephone line, the farmers' phone, went out of existence.

Things change. Now we have a lady minister. I surely didn't ever think we'd have a lady minister. And there's a lot of new people in the church but nowadays if it wasn't for the people that came from the outside and built homes here on the hills we wouldn't have many people left in church.

We had a church officers' meeting. We had one man from the city. But, evidently, city people are altogether different than they are here in the hills. I was concerned about Marvin Stadel. Marvin's storm windows were still on his house. Here it is June and it's hot. And he wasn't really eating right or anything. So I brought it up at this church meeting. I said, "I'm concerned about someone" and I said that it was Marvin. Marvin was the first one if you were in trouble, would be the first one there. If something happened, say a building burned or if you got hurt, Marvin was always the first one there to help.

And now that he needs help himself he's kind of forgotten. That was bugging me. And I said, "I think we should at least see to it that his storm windows are off and maybe we could figure out a way of taking a meal to him once in a while."

This fellow from the city said he wouldn't go and he said, "You're liable to get shot!" And I almost fell over.

I said, "I still think we should help Marvin out a little bit." Wayne Arnold just leaned back in his chair and he said, "When can we go over, Curly?"

I said, "Tomorrow night." So we went over. And there was three happy guys there. Marvin, Wayne, and I. We went to the back door and he let us in and we visited a little while.

Marvin's not driving much, he'll drive down to little George's, but that's about it. He doesn't get to church even. He doesn't know when it's Sunday and he don't know when to eat or anything. He's got Alzheimer's disease pretty bad as his wife, Meta, had. Some people think it's because he's grieving over her.

So we mentioned, "Say, Marvin, you still got your storm windows on."

"Yeah," he said, "And it's getting pretty hot and little Dean isn't big enough to take the storm windows off." Dean is his grandson, little George's son.

We said, "Would you like to have us take them off?"

He said, "Oh, yeah, that would be just fine."

So we took the storm windows off and put the screens on and Marie fixed a little supper for Marvin. I took that over to him when we went over. Anyway, it was still bugging me about this city guy that couldn't see how to help anyone. After church Sunday I said to him, "I wished you could've been along with us the other night to Marvin's. I don't think you'd have had a worry about getting shot."

MARIE: The next time Curly went out to help someone the city guy came along.

CURLY: That reminds me. My dad always told about a fellow that was going to move into a new community. So he went there to visit before he moved there and he went to what would have been one of his neighbors and asked him, "What kind of neighbors will I have around here?"

And the neighbor asks him back, "Well, what kind of neighbors have you got at home?"

"Well," he answers, "They're a bunch of sons-of-bitches!"

And the neighbor tells him, "That's just exactly what you'll have here."

MARIE EVERSOLL

Marie Eversoll was 66 years old when she told her history.

MARIE: Marie Grebner Eversoll was born May 14, 1914 at their farm home in Thompson Township. My childhood was spent on a 100-acre farm with my parents. I was always small. I had every contagious disease. We always went to church every Sunday. On Sunday afternoons Olga played the organ and we would all sing hymns. My father always said the blessing at the table in German. Our financial conditions were—we never had much money but always had plenty to eat.

Some of the church functions were—I was in a three-act play called "The Yellow Shadow" which was sponsored by the young people of the church. I also belonged to the church choir of thirty voices. It was during rehearsal for the play that Curly's and my courtship started. We went together about four years before we were married. It was during the Depression and we had to wait until we had enough money to start housekeeping.

What influenced me most in my choice of spouse was his personality and he was tall, dark, and handsome.

Our first home was two rooms we rented from Henry Boldt, Sr. for $5 a month. We never had much trouble in making ends meet because we never bought anything we didn't have money for. We never bought anything on installment plans, or never used credit cards.

We only had one child, Mary Lou, born December 29, 1939. She was born by cesarean section. After she was born I had a blood clot in my leg which was worse than having a baby. She had a lot of respiratory trouble. She went to grade school at Schapville School, and high school at Scales Mound where she was salutatorian at her graduation. Then she went to the University of Dubuque for one year. Then got married.

I have been a member of Home Extension for 42 years and I have served on the county H.E.A. board for one term. I have belonged to the O.E.S (Order of the Eastern Star) for 15 years and served as Worthy Matron for 22 years. I have taught Sunday school most of the time for 46 years. I am an ordained Deacon-Trustee. I was president of Christian Endeavor before I was married and was church janitor for 20 years.

I had a wonderful father. He was a stonemason, bricklayer, and farmer, and was well liked in the community. My mother was a good seamstress.

Curly's dad was great, too. He was about the kindest person that ever walked the earth. He was a carpenter, mechanic, and electrician. Curly's mother was a hard worker.

My encouragement to my descendants is: Don't buy anything you can't afford, and have a place for everything and have everything in its place, and always have meals ready on time at 12 noon and 5:30 or 6:00 in the evening.

It is eleven forty-five in the morning and a ritual is repeated. Curly walks home from his shop into Marie's kitchen. Marie is carrying a plate with his dinner. At the same moment that he sits down at the table, she puts the plate in front of him. It is twelve noon sharp.

Left: Marie Eversoll cutting her birthday cake. Neighbor Don Gormley looks on.

Less than a mile out of Schapville, west on Stadel Road, is the Boettner homeplace.

It is a high place. Across one hill are the Menzemers and past a field and over another

hill are the Grubes. The Boettners have been in Schapville from the beginning. Ernie

Boettner and Meldon Grube are both related to Anton Schap through the intermediaries

of other families. Meldon's children look to Ernie as a kind of grandfather. So do a lot

of other people.

ERNIE BOETTNER

Ernie Boettner's homeplace is a settler's log cabin that has been "modernized." It has water, siding, smooth walls inside, an indoor toilet, and a basement that Ernie dug out under the house with shovel and pickaxe, carrying sacks of rock and earth out of the front door. When he was born in the house, in 1901, his mother planted a tree near the side of the house that faced the road. He climbed in that tree when he was a child and he leans against it now.

In winter 1954, I turned east off of the old gravel Elizabeth-Scales Mound Road onto the Schapville Road, past the bullet-riddled road sign, to the village. This place was far away from everything. Mine tailings covered the iced and rutted gravel road. I came into Schapville around noon and stopped at the only store, a big barnlike structure which had been Anton Schap's blacksmith shop, now Dave Rury's place. Diesel tractors were parked, running and puffing out white exhaust in the frostbit air. I went in.

A variety of aged chairs, surrounding a round table, bore the weight of farmers who were playing euchre, the town card game, which they stopped when I came in so that they could stare at me. One farmer was thumping the table with his fingers, the tips of two of which were missing. He was the one with the kindest eyes. It was Ernie Boettner. Ernie and I became close friends and neighbors and he told me stories about his life, some of which I tape-recorded while we looked at photographs.

Ernie remembers his wife, Ruth, a beautiful and classy lady.

ERNIE: Ruth taught at the one-room school over there on Hammer Road. Old Bill Hammer went there. She taught Old Bill. Previous to that she taught in the Badlands out there in the Dakotas. She taught out there for a term and then she came back to Dubuque. Her mother was in poor health and when she passed away she came out here and taught. I met her in the Schapville area. I used to see her at church and look for her, so I had the opportunity to meet her personally. And that was it!

Ruth was from Dubuque. When we got close to retirement age we started looking around for a retirement location. We went to different towns. But, she got to love the farm so that no other place seemed suitable and I said, "It kind of looks like you don't like a town anymore." "Well," she said, "I guess that's it."

I always regretted that I wasn't able to give her all the things she deserved, or spend more time with her. She was happy up till a point. I was always too busy farming and doing chores. What I mean is, if you want to make any progress you got to have a certain amount of discontent. We were making progress on the farm but it wasn't enough to make me content. If you are discontented then you'll try to make some headway, you'll try to solve the problem. I enjoyed whatever I was doing and I always looked for better ways of doing it. My wife, too, was always progressing, bettering herself, all the time. It was slow going when you don't have any money. After she had the kids, Joy and Lewis and Jon, she was a full-time farmer's wife. She was a good one! She was 65 when she died. August 1969.

Ruth's cancer had come back after twelve years' remission.

ERNIE: We had quit farming, which was fortunate, so I could put full attention to her, to her care at home. She's buried in the cemetery in our lot. The stone is there. All it needs is my date.

Here's a couple of pictures. I'm 74 there and I'm 28 on the wedding picture. These kind of pictures call attention to what age can do to you. We're not conscious of the years, the numbers. We are, and we are not! It's there, but we don't want to think about it. But our wedding picture is not a hard picture for me to look at. I had a beautiful life with her and we seemed to be quite compatible.

Page 100 and left: Ernie Boettner on his farm.

Above: Ernie Boettner holds a picture of himself with his wife, Ruth.

ERNIE: When I was young I worked in Chicago and that was a pretty good experience. I was a kind of a timid sort of a person, I am now, you know what I mean, up to a point. I got a little more confidence in myself now. Like, once I was invited to a fancy reception in Galena. Different dignitaries from around the area were invited. And I was invited, too! I felt a little bit lost. I was kind of wandering around there and nobody paid any attention to me. So I kind of listened. Everybody was a president of this or a president of that. I kind of thought, well what the hell! So, I kept talking with one guy and I told him I was the president of the local Irish Club! Boy, I was in. Right now! He didn't hear it the way I said it, that I was president of the Liars Club. He didn't hear that part.

I made a deal with my dad to take over the homeplace. In January we moved in. And it was a snow, I guess one of the biggest snows of the history. We had to go through fields, we couldn't use the highways. We used a horse then.

Ernie has a reputation for inventing, cobbling, and making things do. He does not discard wire, old broken tools, metals, wood, or hay binder twine because, "You might need them sometime."

ERNIE: Most farmers put in thirty-five crops in a lifetime. I farmed for thirty-eight years here. It was always changing. I farmed with horses! And then I got a tractor. And then I got other machinery to save labor. I had to. You see, time was the big deal. And if a piece of machinery could take the place of a man I did it right away. I didn't do any different than anybody else. My mechanical ability surely helped me. I only bought two or three pieces of new machinery. I bought used stuff. I had the ability to put them in working order. The size of my place was to my advantage, too. I have a hundred and twenty acres. The tillable farm land is about sixty acres. The rest is pasture. And I never rented any ground. I used to stack hay when I had my barn full. If a machine broke down, I could afford to lose some hay taking the time to fix my machinery.

I ran a kind of experimental place. I'd wonder about ways of doing things and I'd try them out. Sometimes I had luck, and other times it was just a try, a new experience. But it wasn't failure. There isn't any such thing as failure. It's more like experiments that didn't work out.

One time he explained his finger accident.

ERNIE: Farmers are always cutting off a finger, or worse. I was setting up a table saw and I thought I'd run a board through it to test it out. I did a foolish thing. I reached over, behind the saw, and I was going to pull a board through and the saw caught it and fed back. And my hand went through the saw. Oh, it was torn all to hell. See, there's scar tracks all over this finger, the tip of this one is gone, the tip of that one is gone, scar tracks all over this one and even on my thumb. The whole thing was just riddled. Dr. Beauford sewed for two hours. (*He laughs.*) But the thing that I wake up at night and think about is that I could've lost a hand. Oh, that is terrible! But, I tell you, when this happened I thought the end of the world was coming. The shock. And the depression.

Left: Ernie Boettner's neighbors marvelled at his strength.

This page and right: Ernie Boettner mows his pasture, gets an old tractor working again, and talks with Mel Grube, who rents land and buildings from Ernie.

After his accident, Reverend Dexter has to contend with that, too. He has such deep spells of depression. It's shock, that's what it is. You get that when you have an injury. It's the same after surgery. There's the young fellow who lived where Glen Winter lives now, he had some pretty serious surgery. While he was convalescing he had depression. He hung himself.

There have been three or four cases of people hanging themselves in this area that I know about. It's depression that does it. I went through it when I was age fifty-four. There was something wrong. I said to Ruth, "I got to go see a doctor!"

So, I went down to see Doc Speer. He wanted to know how old I was. He says, "I'll fix you up. This is just temporary." And he gave me capsules. I took those for ten years before I got straightened out, I think.

I've had a lot of depression since I came out of the hospital this summer. There are good days and there are some I don't care if "school kept or not." I was going to doctors getting nerve medicine and it helped. I started smoking again and that helped more than anything.

It's depressing about gruesome things happening. Like I heard about where a farmer's heifer was having a calf in amongst the hogs that were around there. While she was calving, the hogs ate the bag off of her and then they ate the calf. And there's been stories where men will have heart attacks in the hog pen. And the men will get eaten. Why, they've eaten kids!

I've had so may funny things happen, too. There's the story of Chrystal and me, how the neighbor caught us both in the bathtub, together!

Here's what happened. She wanted me to finish up her bathroom. Panel it, put ceramics around the tub and all that. I said, "Chrystal, I never did anything like that!" She said, "We can work it out." Well, we were putting ceramics around the bathtub and we were both in the bathtub. She was working here and I was working there and we were working together, y'know. And here, one of the neighbors came in and spread the story about me and Chrystal taking a bath together. Chrystal loves to tell that.

August 15, 1979. Ernie is fixing up the farm, "doing what I couldn't when I was farming." He spends a lot of time reading in a lounge chair set by the window in the living room. At the opposite end of the room is a large mirror which Ernie faces and calls "my rear view window." He reads by the window light and looks in the mirror to see what is going on outside. The window looks out on the tree his mother planted, on the mailbox he cobbled to swing away and back if the road crews hit it, and on his and Meldon Grube's fields. This morning he chain-sawed scrub trees along fence lines. At noon he came in for a dinner of canned foods. Then he read and dozed off.

Right: Ernie looks out his living room window.

Page 111: Ernie Boettner, working a with chain saw, said, "I just don't know when to stop." A neighbor replied, "When you run out of gas!"

Pages 112-113: Ernie outside his house, under the tree his mother planted when he was born.

Summer 1980. Even though he is retired from farming, and living in Freeport with his son, Lewis, and Lewis' wife, Charlotte, Ernie spends a lot of time in Schapville putting his farm in order. Carl and Loren Grube complain that he is working twelve hours a day clearing trees for a fence line. Every year since he recovered from his 1975 heart attack he works hard physically in every kind of weather. "I'm just testing myself," he says.

October 1980. Ernie speaks cheerfully, "Someday they'll find me in the woods. I wish that I had all kinds of time left. Then I could do everything I always wanted to do here. I never had the time when I was farming." He is 79.

July 4, 1982. Ernie says, "It is a beautiful morning in Schapville, every Fourth of July it is more beautiful in Schapville than any place in the world." Until recently, Ernie had been keeping Mrs. Otts company. His expectations for their relationship were dashed when she died. He is 80.

March 1983. Thumping his fingers on the table Ernie said, "Wellll, you know, the barn, why, that's the sign of a farmer! That's like who he is."

Sometimes the thumping of Ernie's finger stumps on the table would make people uneasy.

August 15, 1984. Ernie is on the roof of his house doing new roofing with his sons, Lewis and Jon. A ladder extends from the bed of his truck. A visitor comes around and Ernie says, "I'll be right down," and comes down the ladder and jumps off the truck. The visitor is amazed and declares, "Ernie! How old did you say you are?" He is 83.

April 1986. Driving over the Menzemer Creek and by the hill where his grandfather lived, Ernie says, "The trees that are on the hillside were always there. You walk along that roadway. You take my father-in-law, he dug that roadway by hand. It used to go straight up the hill. Under certain conditions you couldn't get up there. So he built a road around the hill. With a pick and shovel!

"Look at those trees, they've filled in a little bit. By Sunday, with a little warmth, they'll be like real trees. The grass is so green. Oh, this rain is going to do wonders. You get it warm and oh boy! I'm telling you, will the grass come!"

June 23, 1987. Eighty-six-year-old Ernie went into the field to dig postholes. Grube thinks he's putting them in the wrong place, and besides, he says, "It's one hundred degrees in the shade."

Ernie's son, Lewis, drove out from Freeport to check and finds Ernie in the field working on the postholes. He chastises him, takes him back to Freeport, leaving Ernie's blue truck at the farm.

Ernie says, "Lewis grounded me!"

August 20, 1987. Meldon Grube called. "Gordon Elrick died!"

The corn is good on the bottom land along the Apple River. Ernie comes over the bridge and stops his truck. "It was a surprise about my nephew, Gordon. And in New Orleans, Ellis, my son-in-law, Joy's husband, just died of a heart attack. I was just thinking. Things like that come in threes and I think that I'm the next in line."

August 24, 1987. The ashes of Gordon Elrick, age 51, were buried in the Schapville Presbyterian cemetery. Ernie feels uncomfortable about cremation and he wishes Gordon could have had a longer life, "I am having it so good while my friends and relatives are hurting."

February 18, 1988. Ernie stops to see Marvin Stadel at the nursing home. "He didn't know me. It is starting to happen to me. What I did yesterday I've almost forgotten, but what I did twenty-five years ago dominates my thoughts."

May 25, 1988. Ernie is putting in fence to straighten out a pasture line which bordered on Donny Duerr's land.

December 12, 1988. "Besides my memory and hearing loss, otherwise I'm comfortable. Sure is tough when you can't hear, and what you do hear you forget. I've got quite a library now."

March 28, 1989. Ernie will be 88 on April 11. "I went for my driving test and he signed it and I went on to the next desk and the gal gave me a citation for being a good driver. I must have done good on the driving test because I got my license. And I got the hell out of there."

June 5, 1989. Ernie is in the hospital. "This pacemaker is going to be a new experience for me."

August 22, 1989. Ernie is back in the

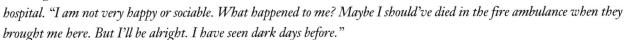

hospital. "I am not very happy or sociable. What happened to me? Maybe I should've died in the fire ambulance when they brought me here. But I'll be alright. I have seen dark days before."

August 24, 1989. He's in a wheelchair in the hospital corridor and he calls the nurse. "I want to show you how I can walk." He gets out of the chair, takes a few steps, becomes breathless, and with a sigh of triumph falls back into the chair. "Just testing," he says.

It is towards the end of September. In the hospital, Lewis and Ernie are together, the son and the father.

Lewis asks, "Are you prepared?"

"For a heck of a long time," Ernie answers.

"Do you think you'll get out of here?" Lewis asks.

"I doubt it," Ernie answers.

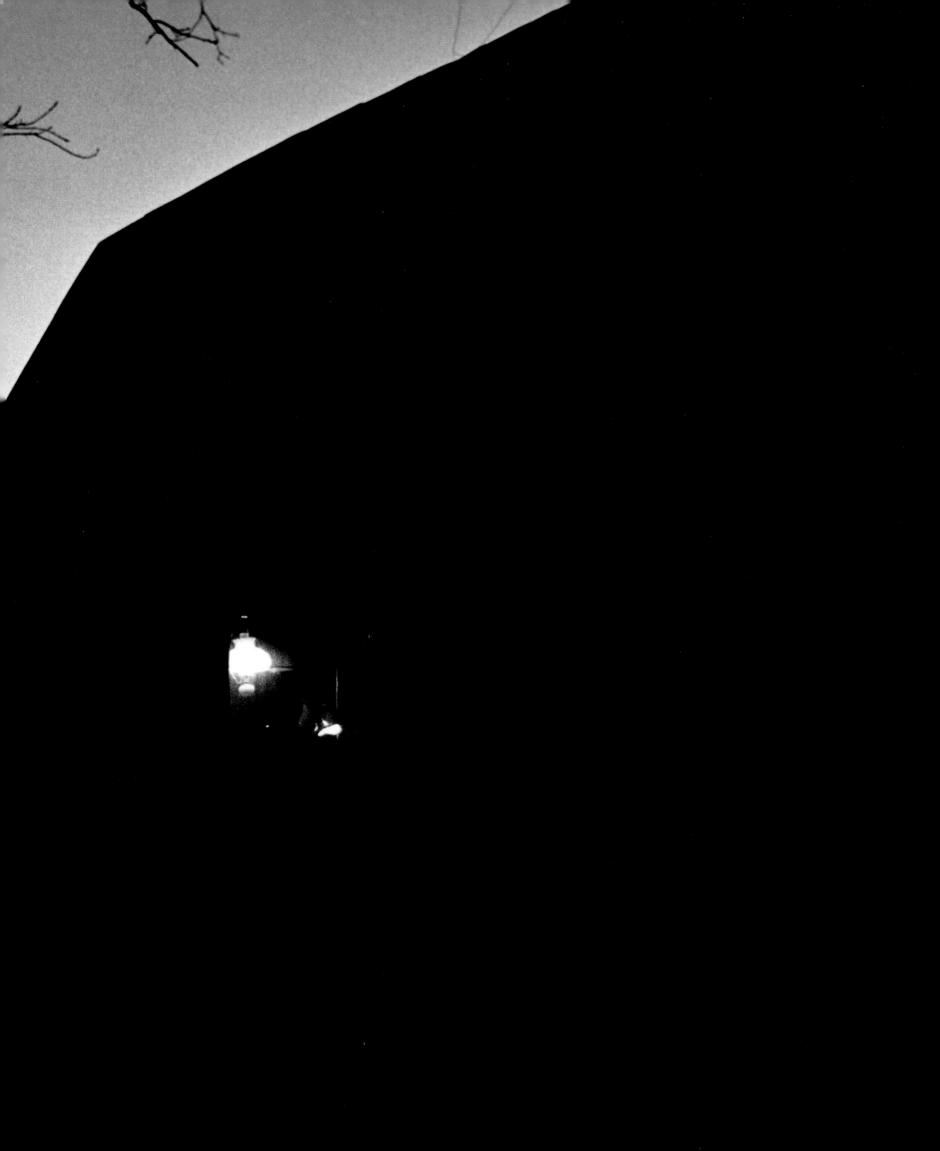

Butch and Connie went together ever since high school in Galena. After they were married in 1972, they moved to Schapville because they liked it there and Butch could farm with Jerry Stadel who was married to Butch's sister, Chrystal. Eventually he bought Jerry Stadel's farm.

He also helped out at the Hammers'. Bill Hammer, Jr. is ten years older than Butch, and Jim Hammer is ten years younger. Butch said that working with them was good and that it was like having a younger brother and an older brother and, in Bill, Sr., a grandfather. Connie said, "Butch farmed at home when he was young and he just loved it. He just has that farming in him. I never want to take that away from him."

BUTCH AND CONNIE MUCHOW

"I was thinking my whole life was going down the tubes. Everything I owned at that time was being sold, was being sold in front of me," remembers Butch Muchow of his farm auction, December 14, 1974.

Connie Muchow adds, "When we started out we were only nineteen and twenty years old. So the trouble we got into maybe was out of a little ignorance. You got to make some mistakes."

It is September 28, 1990. Butch and Connie are talking about those times inside the trailer on the farm they now rent.

BUTCH: The hog market was up to just about sixty dollar hogs and then when I was ready to sell they dropped back down to the forties but all the expenses stayed up high. We had our own hay—enough for the beef cows—and our own corn. But soybean meal and commercial feed was too high for us to operate at a profit.

CONNIE: We went through a period when the pigs kept dying. I had to go in there during the middle of the night and feed them on the bottle—sit there and feed them by hand to try to get them to survive.

BUTCH: We had that MMA disease. The sow's milk would be no good, the sow would actually poison her little pigs when they'd suck so you had to take them off of the sows and feed them cow's milk. It was rough times.

CONNIE: Rather than go in debt we decided we'd better get out.

BUTCH: Even before the auction sale I started helping Bill and Willis out. I was the hired man for years at the Hammers—working with Willis was perfect. I haven't worked with anybody like that since and probably never will. And then when Millie and Willis moved over to Brickners' farmhouse and Bill and Dorothy moved to the Hammer homeplace, we moved to Bill and Dorothy's house in Schapville. We stayed there until 1979.

Cletus and Wilma had moved out to Galena and we moved into their house. Bill had his herd at the homeplace and I had my herd at Cletus and Wilma's and so we decided to put them together and have them all at Bill's and milk in one place instead of two. That's when Bill and Dorothy built their new house on top of the hill over the Hammer homeplace and moved into it. Then we moved from Cletus' over to the Hammer homeplace. That's when Jim got married and he decided to farm on his own and he left home and moved into Cletus and Wilma's with his own herd.

We went all the way on halves with Bill and Dorothy until Bill wanted to get out of milking and into beef. That was after he had his heart attack. We decided we would start looking for a place of our own. We looked around, Bill helped us, and we found this place and we made the deal to rent it and moved here.

CONNIE: We like farming. That's why we're trying to settle here and make it ours. The kids like it here, too. *(Jenny is 7; Jason is 6).*

BUTCH: Our future plans is to buy this farm and build a house.

CONNIE: Yes, buy it, build a house, and live happily ever after.

Page 114: Connie and Butch Muchow

Left: Butch Muchow watching his farm being auctioned off.

117

Top: Neighbors at the Muchows' auction.

Bottom: Connie Muchow at the auction.

Right: It is a cold, raw, and wet December day when the Muchows' machinery and livestock are auctioned off.

JOHN BALBACH, AUCTIONEER

John Balbach became an auctioneer in 1945, when he was an 18-year-old farmer.

JOHN BALBACH: One of the oldest businesses in the world is auctioneering. That's how you get rid of everything. I have sold just about everything from farm machinery to books to hand-carved Japanese ivories called netsuke. I have had auction sales where the family had two or three generations of the original things that the grandfather had bought. Those sales were quite extensive. But you take one like Butch Muchow's sale, that was a long time ago when we were not getting the prices we are today. I think Butch's grain wagon brought thirty-five dollars and his hay elevator went for twenty-five. Butch had not been farming there too long so that he didn't have the average estate most of our auctions have. It's sad when you auction off a young fellow's farm—and his hopes. But, well, you know, farming is a business. And I am a great believer in fate. And if a fellow can't make it farming—whatever the problem—get it over with and go on to the next thing. Don't keep dwelling on something that didn't work for you. I tell them all that I have to auction off, "For heaven's sake, don't get excited about not making this work and don't let anyone give you a bad time by saying that you weren't smart enough. Get it over with and go on with your life." That suggestion is not based on profit for me. I'm a great believer in fate. If something didn't work for you then get on with your life.

I hear that Butch Muchow is farming again and is making progress. Just because we sold him out in '74—because he couldn't make it then—doesn't mean he won't make it now. If he has the willingness to try then he will do it. He's a good example of "don't dwell on something that didn't work for you and get on with your life and the next thing." In his case the next big thing was farming again. He'll make it. He has the willingness. I have never heard a bad word about Butch from anybody. Always says hello to you.

Top left: John Balbach auctioneering the Muchows' farm.

Top center: Auction articles.

Top right: Harvey Gustafson walks down a Scales Mound street with a chair he has just bought at a house auction.

Right: Auction sale in Schapville.

Following pages: Farm auction.

When Meldon Grube was a young man, the neighbors he worked and played with included Curly Eversoll, Ernie Boettner, and Lou Koester. These were the four who one day went around to different parts of their valley, planted dynamite sticks, and exploded them at the same time. Kids around here would do things like that.

There have been Grubes in Schapville since it began. They have given birth, lived, and died in the farmhouse where Meldon is now.

In 1980 Meldon Grube, age 55, became part of the farm crisis.

Now it is the winter of 1984. It is early morning and after breakfast in the Grube farmhouse. Meldon Grube is closing diaper pins alongside the zipper that no longer works on the tattered, hooded red sweatshirt he is wearing. He puts a jacket on over that, and then one-piece coveralls over that and then his tall rubber chore overshoes over his boots. He puts on his winter cap, pulls the flaps down over his ears, puts the hood over that and a scarf around that, which also covers his nose and mouth. It is twenty-two degrees below zero with a wind-chill factor of minus forty. He used to like the combat of the winters and the work and the dressing for it. But today it all seems useless. "Forty years useless," says Meldon.

He and Loren, dressed in a like fashion, are going out to do the chores, feed the cattle, and check the water. For a moment he pauses in the doorway to read the landscape. In that moment he sees the wind making leafless branches and tree limbs dance. He sees three-foot snow drifts. He sees animal tracks. He hopes that drifting snow has not covered the lanes he bladed out yesterday. He hopes that the water is not frozen and that he will not have to fix broken pipelines and he hopes that he will not find any sick or dead cattle. He straightens up, looks around the room, and turns back to his son.

"Come on Loren, let's go. It's time to be a farmer!"

Meldon and Loren leave the house. Dozing on the pine floor is Duchess, the Australian sheepdog.

Meldon was born in this house in an upstairs bedroom which he now uses as an office. Except for two years, when he lived in Nora, Illinois, fifteen miles away, this house has always been his home. In this house, Meldon's grandfather and his mother were born. In this house, Evelyn and Meldon raised eight children: Chuck, Jane, Joyce, twins Leah and Loren, Donny, Carl, and David. One baby, who was Jane's twin, died at birth. They put four of them through college, those that wanted to go. In this year, only three of the boys are at the homeplace: Carl, a construction worker, Loren, and David, a high-school student. Of all the children, Loren is the only one who farms full-time with Meldon.

Meldon and Evelyn have devoted their lives to the children, the farm, and the land. But no longer are there ten people rushing around. Those times are gone and, except for visiting grandchildren, the house is quiet. It is a house with a comfortable history. It was built in 1880 by great-grandmother Brickner. The farm was settled in 1855, one hundred and twenty years ago, before the Civil War, when great-grandfather George Grube owned most of Schapville including the church land.

In 1984 Meldon is fifty-nine years old.

January 1985. The temperature is a warm forty degrees. Meldon stops by, opens the door of the pickup and shows me a load of shotguns and rifles. He has just come from Curly Eversoll's workshop and from Ernie Boettner's farm where, for safety, he had stashed all this ordnance. There is optimism and a great idea in his look.

MELDON: I want to show you something. Bet you never saw anything like this! It's a Colt 22-caliber repeating rifle. It's rare. Winchester was supposed to make rifles and Colt was supposed to make the revolvers. I'm going to clean them up and bring them to Freeport to be appraised. No use having them around when I need the cash more. Especially when it might mean that I can hold on to the farm a little longer. Here is one I'm going to try to hold on to. It was my grandfather's shotgun and he gave it to me on my eighteenth birthday. I fired it that day, too. We looked up to the ridge and there were these deer running along. I'm going to try to hold on to this shotgun.

Page 124: Mel Grube at Jackie Duerr's auction.
Right: Mel Grube pinning hooded sweatshirt before going out into a snowstorm.

Meldon is a big man. At rest he appears to be a stern man whose hazel eyes do not betray his inner feelings. These days the smiles are quick and brief. There are bursts of unexpected anger. Like most farmers around Schapville, he can fix all kinds of machinery, put thousands of dollars of seed and fertilizer into the ground confidently, and get good crops. He plows a straight furrow and once told Georgie Stadel, the road commissioner, "Don't you ever take out that old oak stump by the side of the road, it's my marker." He can lift a two-hundred pound weight, heal a sick animal with medicine or a blade. He can ring pigs and castrate the meat animals.

Now he looks around and asks a neighbor, "What will happen to us all in this second depression?" He considers selling the farm. "I would have to pay taxes on what I would get out of the sale, and I would still owe the Farm Credit System and I would be short. I have already borrowed on my insurance and I don't have an appreciable government pension because I never had enough to contribute and I have no savings left."

Early March, 1986. The Farm Credit System is going broke and so are small towns, their banks, and farmers. President Reagan declares that the federal government "helped get these folks in trouble and we're not going to pull the rug out from under them while they're struggling to get back on their feet."

Meldon tries to get loans, works at a nearby ski jump as a guard, does farming for others, puts up grain bins, and runs his own farm.

MELDON: The Farm Credit System decided to change the rules in the middle of the game. They made us go to a variable interest rate. What was supposed to be a couple of points higher in our interest rate doubled and turned out to be 16 percent to 17 percent. We were paying an interest bill equal to what we had agreed or planned to pay for interest and principal. Because of the policy which the Farm Credit System imposed on us and others like us we had to start changing plans. We sold off assets which reduced our farm earning power and so we started to construct and sell grain storage buildings. This was good until the government decided not to put out any more money for farm storage. So this dried up, but I continued to try to sell farm-related equipment until farm prices dropped to the point where farmers didn't have any money for this type of thing. There was sickness in the family and we had to cut back on acres as well as reduce the amount of livestock. When we would not do away with the good soil conservation practices we had been doing for forty years they called in our operating loan. At that point we were marked as one of the 10 percent of farms which are to be closed out each year for the next three years.

I agreed to have a sale at the end of November. We couldn't get the corn out until late and the party that wanted to rent the farm couldn't get operating money. So by getting money with cheaper interest from another source and cashing part of my life insurance we were able to hold things together.

In 1986, we decided to put the farm up for sale after paying off the FHA loan, and paying the Farm Credit System's loan — about $25,000 in principal and interest. We should have another $25,000 to $30,000 within the next five months toward paying them off but they don't want less than the WHOLE THING. The Farm Credit System don't want to do business with someone my age.

Left: During the annual family picnic, the immediate Grube family poses for a picture. *First row, left to right:* Donny, Jayne, Joyce; *second row:* Evelyn, Loren, Chuck, Leah; *third row:* Meldon, David, Carl.

Above: Porch of the Grube homeplace.

Following pages: Victor Sprengelmeyer (Meldon Grube's lawyer) and Meldon Grube waiting in creditor's meeting room.

Meldon is now sixty-one years old.

November 1987. Meldon and Evelyn receive a notice of imminent foreclosure. A neighbor's letter to Pastor Donna, the Grube's minister, is circulated at church. It asks that the congregation call the vice president of the Farm Credit System and ask him to reconsider the foreclosure and forbearance application. It concludes: "Meldon Grube has been a vital force in this community and in his church. We know him as a man that is all we seek in a friend and neighbor and who holds those virtues we like to think the American farmer practices as faith."

There are so many calls that the credit agency reconsiders. Meldon meets with his current credit officer. The everchanging credit officers have to familiarize themselves with Meldon's thick files. To Meldon, their letters never reflect the conversations they have in the office. His credit officers disappear, shifted elsewhere in the system or, Meldon thinks, they resign because they are farm people who are in anguish over foreclosing on other farmers.

Meldon is 62 now.

1988. Drought. One-tenth of an inch of rain falls between April and July. The fields are low on moisture. Meldon and his neighbors put in their crops and hope for the best. The grass is brittle. Walking on it grinds it to dust.

Loren says, "Delmar Dittmar says we should go out and prime the fields with a glass of water so that when the rain comes it would soak down."

Corn can send roots down twenty feet to seek out moisture but there is no moisture. Usually there is an average of one hundred bushels to an acre. Some fields yield only thirty bushels. It is the same for all the crops. Meldon sells off two tractors.

Now he's 63.

It is 1989. Land value in Jo Daviess County is going up and farm prices are going down. Farmers are selling their land and going out of business. Not out of business, but worried, Meldon says, "If a depression comes at least we will be able to eat."

Meldon is sixty-four years old.

1990. The snow leaves moisture in the ground and there is rain enough to give the crops a good start. The drought is over.

MELDON: I'm looking for some sort of vehicle to keep the farm to turn it over to the next generation. If I sell some of the herd and other things, if my land is reappraised right it should be enough to get another loan from a bank to pay off the Farm Credit System. With less interest on the new loan the farm could support the payments.

The next generation of Grubes is scattered. Chuck is in Florida, Donny is in Wisconsin, Jane is in Iowa, Joyce is also in Iowa not far from Jane, Leah is in California. Carl, David, and Loren, who still works the farm with Meldon, all live in the county. Meldon and Evelyn have twelve grandchildren.

On July 1, the Grubes have their annual family picnic and all the children and their families come back to the homeplace. Ernie Boettner and a few other neighbors are not here, but Louie Koester is. With all the grandchildren there are plenty of people.

On July 4, Carl climbs on top of a grain bin to fix the roof and falls off. His elbow tears through the skin and he breaks his wrist. Veins and arteries are cut. Carl is in surgery three and one half hours. Pastor Donna rushes to the hospital. Helen Kilgore, who drove the volunteer ambulance the thirty miles to the Dubuque hospital, thinks it is through the grace of God that Carl's arm and life are saved.

In August there are flash flood warnings. The corn is very high. The soybeans are dealer perfect, but too much rain prevents an abundance of beans. What is needed now is ninety-degree weather.

It is late in August 1990. In the homeplace after supper the dishes have been done and Meldon is in his chair. Loren and Evelyn are at the dining room table watching the television news from Iraq. The weather has been hot and humid and they are exhausted from the work of the day. Today's mail brought the Farm Credit System's foreclosure letter. A breeze is coming through the house. Dozing on the pine floor is Duchess, their Australian sheep dog, who seems unmindful of the past ten years.

It is 1990 and Meldon Grube is sixty-five years old.

Pages 132-133: Meldon Grube watches while representatives of his lender take an account of his assets for their "Farm Property List."

Left: Loren Grube brings grain to my horses.

Following pages: The Grube homeplace.

THE CEMETERY

August 27, 1977. Old Bill Hammer was buried in the cemetery of the Schapville Zion Presbyterian Church a few weeks after the Ice Cream Social. The church in its rolling landscape with its steeple and unfenced cemetery is what a country church should look like. It is a place from a common past. It is a loved place. Since 1983 Donna Wrzescz (pronounced Resh) has been pastor and lives in the manse with her husband, Owen.

MARIE EVERSOLL: The church was organized in 1854 by fifty people who had come from Bavaria and Württemberg, Germany. One of those people was Old Bill Hammer's great-grandfather. They were almost kind of like Mennonites and they met first on Hammer's Bottom by the Mill Creek and then on account of the building being too small and the creek getting too dangerous to cross they moved to that rock—Schoenhart School on the ridge. That's where the church was organized with Presbyterian service by students from the seminary in Dubuque. But then, the ridge was too far to go so they met over there at Ernie Boettner's until they had money enough to build a log church and finally moved the church from Boettners' to George Grube's land right in Schapville. They spoke in German at their services up until the Second World War.

The church is at the west side of the village at the confluence of Schapville, Hoppe, and Stadel roads. Its bell is still rung by hand with a thick hemp rope. Aunt Emma Hammer used to ring it. She died shortly after she retired and the doctor wrote on the certificate "Died of not having the church bells to ring." And here, Ernie Boettner, born in 1901, learned his favorite hymn, "Just As I Am." He hopes to have it sung at his burial. Ernie remembers his grandfather, Joseph Schwartz, ringing the bell. George Stadel rang it for the one-hundredth anniversary service because his father, Marvin, who was supposed to, was ill. The steeple is topped by a neon cross which Millie Gormley said is the town's nightlife, along with the lights of the Pepsi-Cola machine a couple of hundred yards to the east of the front of the church, outside of Anton Schap's original blacksmith shop, now owned by Carmine Panico. Across the Schapville Road to the north of the church is Bill Hammer, Jr.'s land, where he and Dorothy had their first house.

Henry Hoppe's house is to the south of the church on Stadel Road. Next door, on the corner of Hoppe and Stadel, directly across the road from the church, where in November of 1988 they celebrated their fiftieth wedding anniversary, is Curly and Marie Eversoll's house. Lace curtains and lamps are in the two picture windows of the parlor. Between them is the never-used front door. Neighbors use the kitchen door. The oval-shaped glass in the front door frames the church and the cemetery, where the Eversolls' monument is already set, and suggests that this is the way things are supposed to be.

More than two hundred-and-fifty people are buried in the cemetery. Families and neighbors put flowers on the graves and comment:

"When I go by I remember relatives and friends I played with, fought with, worked with, shared memories with, and ate with."
"This is a religious place and people make a place religious by carrying their dead into it."
"This place and all that are buried here should be loved because if they are loved they are remembered and are with us forever."
"Because if you remember then that's like their resurrection."
"The cemetery, why, it's the homeplace, for the living or dead, to come back to, to be with family and neighbors."
Ernie Boettner's wife, Ruth, is buried here. Ernie said, "You ought to be buried in the place that was home."

On a very cold and clear February morning, a lot of jack-hammering noise coming from the cemetery brought Chrystal Stadel and her daughter Tammy (age 6) and Chrystal's brother, young farmer Butch Muchow, to watch the gravediggers from Vincent's of Galena finish breaking the ground through the frost. When Butch asked who the grave was for, Chrystal answered, "It's someone I didn't know—it was someone that had moved away a long time ago—and like most people from the town that die, has come back to be buried at home."

"How far down have you got?" Butch then asked the Vincent men.

"Three feet."

"Oh, then you got three more feet to go, don't you?" Butch asked.

"No. Another foot."

"But I thought you guys dig a grave six feet deep," Butch said.

"Not in the winter."

It was the end of the summer of '77 when Old Bill Hammer was in the hospital. Mildred said, "They told him that there was no longer any hope and that all that they could do was to make him comfortable. Bill just said to the doctors, 'Uh huh, yes, I understand. Thank you, doctor.' When the doctor left, Bill shook a little and I said to him, 'You had some hope before he told you that, didn't you dear?' 'Yes,' he said, and turned over and slept."

In April at corn-planting time, Bill had found out about his cancer. Now in August, when the corn had matured, he was dead. He was 63.

The winter of 1976-1977 was severely cold. Old Bill did not feel very well. His breath was short and he had little energy. He said, "As soon as spring comes I'll be better again." In character, Bill said nothing more.

When April came he was feeling so bad, he told Millie he was hoping that he would die and they went to the doctor. Though x-rays that had been taken a year before revealed nothing, the doctors now saw a tumor. Bill went home to wait for surgery later in the month. Home was now at the Brickner farm, around the hill from the Hammer homeplace where Bill, Jr. and Dorothy now lived. The Brickners lived above the grocery they operated in Scales Mound. Millie had a new plan when the Brickners sold the store to Pat and Sheila Ohms. Millie's idea was to buy a house in Scales Mound in which she and Bill could live and he could still do chores at the farm. They bought the house and Millie had started to fix it up when Bill got sick.

Bill was never without a cigarette; now Bill was forbidden to smoke, but he smoked when Millie was in town hurrying to fix the house. Before she returned he hid his ashtray and cigarettes from her. I smoked with him. Smoking with him now was not a casual act but was spiritual, a kind of ritual, an act of defiance—for if normal things were done, wouldn't everything be normal?

After Bill's surgery Janet Brickner telephoned: "Dad's been operated on for the lung cancer. It was inoperable and they immediately sutured him up."

Mildred and Janet were busy at the house. Mildred said, "I'm trying to get the house done as soon as possible so that me and Bill could live there together. Then I could always say that it was ours."

Bill's biggest complaint: "If a fellow could just do a little of what he used to it would be O.K. I used to be able to pick up the pieces for Mildred when things went wrong. Now I can't."

When Bill and Mildred moved from Brickner's farm to the house in town it was the first time that Bill had lived anywhere else other than in the valley in which he was born.

Not long after that he was brought to the Galena hospital. He got oxygen but was confused about where he was. Mildred told him: "You are in the hospital, dear."

"Good. That's just the way I like it, it's just where I want to be." Bill died at 7:30 P.M. on August 25.

Now it is Friday night, August 26, and the crowded visitation is in the large, high-ceilinged rooms of the Steinke Funeral Home's historic Galena mansion. Close to him, his family is receiving condolences.

Mildred tells one neighbor, "Just before his last breath he looked awful. With that last breath he relaxed and looked peaceful. The way he looks right now is the way he looked a moment after he died. The undertaker didn't make him look that way. It was the way he looked after he died—peaceful. I'm glad that Junior was there at the bedside with me, otherwise he would never have believed me."

When it is time to go, Mildred tells one lingering neighbor, "I'll never see him again after tonight. I would just like to take him home with me now. Even when he was sick and sleeping I knew he was there and I could touch him. I know he is with God, and I have his spirit with me, but I won't ever have his arms around me again."

The next day, August 27, a hot and humid one (the kind the corn likes), with all the pews filled, the funeral was held at the Schapville Zion Presbyterian Church. Bill and Mildred were married here on September 19, 1934.

When the service was over, casketbearers Carl Haenert, Cletus Hammer, Oscar Krug, Elmer Krug, Butch Muchow, and Vernon Virtue carried the coffin out the front door, around the church to the cemetery, and to the grave and the tent that was over it. Their women carried the flowers to Old Bill's grave.

After the burial, everyone came in from the graveyard to the church for a lunch. Mildred said, "Last night we all said goodbye to Bill. Junior got them all to let me be alone with Bill. Why go through it again today, what we did in the funeral home last night? That was a private family affair when we were alone with him and the coffin was open. We all said goodbye then. And so when we came into the church the coffin was closed."

In another year, on the first Thursday in August, the famous Schapville Zion Presbyterian Church Annual Ice Cream Social will be held. In the afternoon, people will come from miles around to eat homemade pies and ice cream, barbecued beef, fried chicken, beans, coleslaw, potato salad, marshmallow Jell-O salad, mostly made by the church ladies. By twilight there will be skits, and gospel and country music on a hayrack platform stage outside the altar door and by the edge of the cemetery; wooden planks set on square hay bales will serve as seats. Some people will stroll along the gravestones. There will be applause and laughter and talk about weather and crops. After a prayer of thanks, people will go to their cars, parked on Hoppe and Stadel and Schapville roads, and leave. Then this place will be still again. Waiting. Waiting for neighbors to come home to this religious place, to this homeplace.

Left: Family on the cemetery lawn.
Top: Ernie Boettner is served by Curly Eversoll.
Bottom: Ice Cream Social.
Pages 146-147: Evening, Ice Cream Social.

Joel Dexter and Elaine Hammer

Earl Winter of Schapville

Dance in Donny Duerr's new barn.

Chris Stadel

Pastor Donna

Don Duerr, David and Kathy Dittmar, and Donna and Gerald Morhardt at the Ice Cream Social.

Scales Mound celebrates its 130th anniversary with a town barbecue.

Neighbors scrape paint off St. John's Lutheran Church on the Elizabeth-Scales Mound Road.

George Stadel ringing the church bell.

Laura and Laverne Grebner and grandchild.

Schapville Zion Presbyterian Church

Church service.

George Stadel at church Ice Cream Social.

The church's annual Ice Cream Social.

THE SILENT LAND

Sunday, August 28, 1977. Bill had been in his grave for a day. It is cloudy, hot, and humid. It is raining. I go to make pictures, but I am too sad to make pictures of the land that he had just left, a silent land, an empty landscape, because I think I will never see Bill in it again. There are flowers on his grave. One bouquet has a banner that says "Neighbors." Men from the church club are playing horseshoes and throwing a baseball around in the graveyard. At his house, Ernie Boettner is reading;

Meldon Grube is "fixing fence" that a cow had gone through; a lot of other neighbors are napping after Sunday dinner. And young Bill Hammer is doing the evening milking and chores.

August 31, 1977. Mildred is in her kitchen. She wants to make breakfast and talk. "Lots of people gave money in Bill's memory. Maybe we'll use it for the cancer fund and maybe buy some trees for the church where the old ones died. Or maybe a piano for the church."

She offers a piece of cake and says, "I have been thinking about what some ministers say: 'Have faith. Have faith and everything will be all right.' Does that mean that there are a lot of faithless people in the cemetery?"

Mildred goes to the coffeepot and comes back with another thought, "I know that the grave has an empty shell. And I know Bill is with God."

After a silence she says, "Walter was here and asked if I minded if he took Bill's clothes. And here is a few I bundled for you."

Since Bill's death people have been staying with her. Now she says, "I've got to start being alone and start that fight!"

September 4, 1977. Sunday. Labor Day weekend. The dryness of September had quickly knifed through the humidity of the week before. It is a bright day, but the kind in which eyes can rest in the serenity of the light. The winds caress the face, surround it and move on. There is always a nice wind up here on the old Hoppe place. Bill rested here and smoked and drank lemonade under the trees on hot days when he was putting square bales of hay up in the barn. With Bill's death much of what was Jo Daviess County for me went with him and what I had come to photograph was gone. This day with its deep blue sky and puffs of white clouds has changed that forlorn idea. It is a beautiful day. I load my camera. No person who anyone has ever known and loved really leaves.

December 1978. It is a little over a year since Old Bill's death. It is Sunday and after church Mildred walked to the edge of the cemetery. She said, "I wanted to go over to Bill's grave. I missed him and I will keep missing him, but the snow was so deep. And it was time to stop mourning. Besides, like it says in the Bible, 'It came to pass.' It didn't say 'It came to stay.'"

Left: Mildred Hammer, widowed five years, on the porch of her Scales Mound house.

Above: At the Ice Cream Social, my grandsons, Seth and Taylor, pass by Bill Hammer, Sr.'s grave.

Following pages: View of the church and cemetery from the Eversolls' front parlor.

EPILOGUE

Powerful forces led me first to the Hammers and then to the neighbors and suggested that the qualities I witnessed in their lives—strength, goodness, harmony, universal order—were worth preserving. Out of friendship alone, nothing more, they consented to become my allegories for those things. In authentic ways, their lives say for me what I cannot say without them about the spiritual and the American heritage of farm families and rural life.

With them and with other fragments of experience, I have learned that what I was taught as a child is, or can be, mostly true. I learned that there has been only one true creative act, the making of something out of nothing, an act performed only by the sole Creator. All else is circumstance, experience, invention, innovation, discovery—more than anything else—and a putting together in a particular fashion of things that have always existed. Perhaps every act and every discovery, as Bill Hammer, Jr. would say "was meant to be."

Left: Jayne Grube on her wedding day.
The children of friends pose with her.

Mildred Hammer measuring Bill Hammer, Jr. at age 14, June 1955.

Age 18, September 1959.

Age 29, August 1974.

Age 44, July 1985.

Afterword

Willis A. Hammer, Jr.

Born April 8, 1941. Died December 27, 1990.

Within a year of his father's death in August 1977, Young Bill had open-heart surgery. He continued to work the farm for thirteen years, until his heart failed and he died in Mercy Hospital, Dubuque, Iowa, on December 27, 1990. He told his daughter, Jayne, who was visiting him in the hospital, "It ain't so bad to die."

The wake was held in the funeral home in Scales Mound which had been The Flamingo Tea Room where Bill and Millie celebrated their twenty-fifth wedding anniversary and where Bill and Dorothy celebrated their wedding-day dinner. The funeral services were held in the First Presbyterian Church in Scales Mound, the church Bill and Dorothy attended and in which they were married. The church was completely filled with mourners, some standing. Internment was in the Schapville Zion Presbyterian Church Cemetery in the family plot. Surviving are his wife, Dorothy; his son, Jim, who farms nearby in Wisconsin and who has two daughters and one son; his daughters Jayne and Judy, who is married and has one son; his sister, Janet; and his mother, Mildred.

Young Bill had given up the dairy operation and gone into beef production. A week before his death he sold the homeplace.

Six weeks later, February 8, 1991. On Hammer's other hay field on Schapville Road big hay rolls are being loaded on a truck trailer bed. Young Bill's last crop was going to a cattle operation in Lanark, Illinois. The driver said, "I guess the old farmer died. They're selling off everything."

Mildred Hammer

Born April 16, 1916. She died on Mother's Day, Sunday May 9, 1993 at her home in Scales Mound.

After a debilitating three-year illness, she stopped medical treatment, food and water and died within the week. She succumbed gracefully and when she spoke she was kind to us.

The wake was held in Scales Mound in the former Flamingo Tea Room. Burial was in the Schapville Zion Presbyterian Church between her husband Willis Hammer, Sr., and her son, Willis Hammer, Jr.

Surviving are her daughter Janet (Mrs. Bill Brickner), seven grandchildren and nine great-grandchildren.

"You better come out." Millie Hammer had beckoned us into her neighborhood twenty years ago. We came and we started Neighbors. *Editing on this book was concluded and the text went to the printer at the time of her death.*

Marie Eversoll

Born May 14, 1914. Died June 10, 1989.

"Marie Grebner Eversoll died Saturday June 10, 1989," read the notice in The Weekly Visitor. "Services were held Tuesday afternoon at Schapville Zion Presbyterian Church. Burial was in the church cemetery. Mrs. Eversoll was a homemaker."

At the funeral the church is filled and there is spillover into the activities room where Curly and Marie had recently held their fiftieth wedding anniversary celebration.

HALDOR SCHAP

Haldor Schap died December 28, 1990. He was seventy-four years old.

HENRY HOPPE

Henry Hoppe died February 4, 1985, three months short of his ninety-sixth birthday. Marie Eversoll said of her neighbor, "He was ready and looking forward to it. An hour after he said, 'I'm tired, so tired. My time has come. It will be over soon,' he rolled over and went to sleep."

The Hoppe name was gone from Schapville except on the road signs and the gravestones in the Lutheran cemetery.

RICKY STEGALL

Ricky Stegall picks up milk from farmers in a milk truck he drives for a dairy. He lives in Jo Daviess County. He is married and has four children.

MELDON GRUBE

On October 20, 1992, Meldon Grube secured a loan from the Elizabeth State Bank to pay off the Farm Credit System. The board was composed of neighbors who looked favorably on Meldon. John Balbach, acting as Meldon's agent, will sell the real estate, the proceeds of which will be used to pay off the bank. Curly Eversoll has arthritis problems, so early every morning, before his chores, Meldon checks in on Curly, his neighbor.

BUTCH AND CONNIE MUCHOW

1992. The Muchows have purchased the farm that they had been renting.

JOEL DEXTER

Joel Dexter is married to Wendy and they live in downstate Illinois. After working on newspapers as a photographer, Joel now works for the State of Illinois Geological Survey. He comes back frequently to Schapville.

ERNEST BOETTNER

Born April 11, 1901. Died October 14, 1989.

The high color of autumn lasts but a week. When farmer Ernie Boettner died on October 14, 1989, at 6:30 A.M., his final hour came during a day of appropriately intense autumn color. His funeral was on October 16 at the Schapville Zion Presbyterian Church. Pastor Donna conducted the service. Burial was in the church cemetery next to his wife, Ruth. The pallbearers were Meldon Grube, Jack Elrick, Ed Boettner, Hal Schap, Verle Stadel, Donny Duerr, Hal Boettner, Curly Eversoll, Georgie Stadel, and me.

Following pages *(left to right)*: Tammy Stadel, Tommy Wasmund, Jerry Stadel, and Butch Muchow

There is serenity now in a place I know like no other. It is around Scales Mound in the deeply etched panorama of Jo Daviess County, in the northwest corner of Illinois, where the land is crayon green in the spring and fleece white in the winter, and stays that way until the thaw.